EMPOWERED WOMEN IN BUSINESS

Inspiration And Advice From 21 Empowered Women Entrepreneurs

Table of Contents

INTRODUCTION

Don't just stand for the success of other women – insist on it."

—Gail Blanke, President, and CEO, Lifedesigns

As women, whenever we enter a new phase of life; as a wife, a mother, or grandmother, we tend to lean on one another for support and counsel for the new challenges each phase presents. This sisterhood has been the backbone of many friendships and has empowered women in homes across diverse cultures for ages. Still, we have just as much to offer in business and to the economy as we do in homes. If we have learned to draw support from one another regarding home-related or personal issues, how much more in business.

When women come together and seek to collaborate rather than compete, we can multiply our power to create a monumental impact. Research has shown that an economy not empowering women to thrive in business is shortchanged. The success of women in business has a ripple effect on the economy and community both locally and globally. The number of women in business is steadily growing; with 114% more today than 20 years ago.

For women, the challenges posed by the largely male-dominated industries, poor access to funding, fear of failure, self-doubt, inadequate knowledge of work-life balance, and the lack of models and mentors for women make entrepreneurship appear daunting. These discourage women from starting businesses and slow the growth of the many who have already started a business.

Empowering Women in Business was birthed to provide a means for women to navigate the barriers we face in business and create a community of women supporting one another and using our combined resources to create, grow and scale our business to levels beyond imaginable success.

In this book, Selena Dorsey, founder of Empowered Women Publishing and Empowered Women In Business Summits, teams up with 21 exceptional and prominent women entrepreneurs from across various industries, ethnicities, and family backgrounds to share their experiences and how they have successfully navigated the uncharted terrain of building a business. Each person's story is unique, just as yours will be, but they are also relatable and contain practical wisdom that can be easily applied.

This book will provide a roadmap, showing you how to approach each obstacle you encounter, it will inspire you to step up to the arduous but equally rewarding task of building a business and encourage you to forge forward in every season of your business.

Are you ready to; learn how to hold your own in a male-dominated field, gain access to more funding, silence the voice of fear and doubt, join a community of women thriving in business and flourish in every aspect of your life? if yes, this book is for you. A whole new world of opportunities and success awaits you.

SELENA DORSEY

Lifestyle Entrepreneur & Virtual Summit Expert

https://www.selenad.com

https://www.crushitwithsummits.com

https://www.empoweredwomensummit.net

Selena D. is a Lifestyle Entrepreneur & Virtual Summit Expert.

Selena D. is the expert for helping entrepreneurs like you craft profitable and successful Virtual Summits that allow your business to reach more people, make a greater impact, and establish yourself as the go-to authority in your industry. Her signature program, Crush it With Summits, is the Gold Standard training for business owners looking to create 5 & 6-figure virtual summits.

The Power Of Virtual Summits

By Selena Dorsey

In March of 2020, I was on the Gold Coast in Australia readying to host my in-person conference for hundreds of coaches. I had just flown in after a long flight from New York City and was eager to meet and greet everyone that made it, including my Australian partner, event volunteers, and conference speakers and attendees.

Little did I know that in just 24 hours, I would receive an urgent message from my travel agent that the United States was gearing up to close its borders because of COVID-19 and I needed to get on the first flight back home.

As you can imagine, I was devastated!

If you've ever hosted an in-person event, you know that it can take up to a year to plan, with all of the costly and time-consuming elements that go into the organizing, logistics, and coordination. So the thought of all my hard work over the past year being wasted was inconceivable to me and totally deflating. I wanted to put my face in my hands and cry.

After feeling sorry for myself for about an hour, I sprung into action. I met up with my Australian partner to let her know my situation and that I had to leave. I packed up my things, checked out, and headed to the airport.

On the long flight home, I thought about my health and also my business. I thought about how this was the beginning of something that might shake up the world. A few days after I returned, countries began to close their borders and businesses began to shut down. We were in a full-blown pandemic. My in-person conference business that I had built up over the years, was now in limbo and I had two choices: sink or swim. I chose to swim.

I got together with my team and we came up with a strategy and a plan to move forward. And that plan was virtual summits. I had never hosted or even thought of hosting a virtual summit before the pandemic and suddenly that seemed like our only option. However, I knew time was of the essence and there was no room for mistakes, so I hired the best virtual summit consulting firm to teach me the ins and outs of profitable virtual summits.

For the next few months, my team and I worked feverishly to get this done. There were lots of all-nighters and sleepless nights to pull off the impossible. In June of 2020, less than three months since the world had changed, we hosted our very first virtual summit- and it was a huge success!

We had 50+ speakers from around the world and thousands of participants tuning in. We were amazed at how well it was received and intrigued by how well it worked! Since then, we have hosted over a dozen profitable virtual summits and helped others create their own.

In the two years since, I sometimes wonder what would have happened had the pandemic never occurred. Would I still be traveling the globe hosting in-person conferences? I don't know the answer to that, but what I do know is that magical things can happen when you don't give up and when you don't quit.

Virtual summits saved me. Saved my business. And I am eternally grateful. And you can unlock the same success with one of your own, in whatever industry you come from.

Want to create a profitable virtual summit for your business? Sign up for our Crush It With Summits Masterclass here: https://www.crushitwithsummits.com

SHARON M. JURD

International No. 1 Best-Selling author / Seasoned Business Executive / Entrepreneur / Growth Strategist / Success Coach

https://smjcoachinginstitute.com

https://www.instagram.com/sharonjurd/

https://web.facebook.com/sharonmareejurd

Sharon is a highly respected international No. 1 best-selling author as well as a seasoned Business Executive, Entrepreneur, Growth Strategist, and Success Coach.

She is passionate about helping people grow their business faster than the competition by giving business owners, just like you, financial freedom and the choice to live the life they deserve.

Sharon is the Director of her own international franchise 'HydroKleen', now in over 45 countries. She is the founder of SMJ Coaching Institute where she teaches, coaches, and mentors coaches to grow their businesses. Sharon is a Director of 9 companies and her professional achievements have been recognized by winning over 36 industry awards including the most sought after, Australian Franchise Woman of the Year.

For more than 20 years, Sharon has worked, traveled, consulted, and taught internationally, speaking to and motivating thousands of people.

Sharon's achievement and motivational programs have been published in newspapers and magazines nationally, and internationally, and have made her a sought-after speaker and consultant on the international stage.

She is the international author of the book "How To Grow Your Business Faster Than Your Competitor" and her latest book "Extraordinary Women in Franchising". Sharon is accredited with the International Board of Hypnosis and the International Board of Time Line Therapy® as a Master Practitioner, Coach, and Trainer.

She is world-renowned for her strategies for business growth, sales and marketing, franchising, coaching and speaking, self-development, and accelerated psychological transformation.

She lives in Queensland, Australia with her husband John.

5 Simple Steps To Freedom & Success

By Sharon Maree Jurd

I was 29 years of age, married with two small children aged four and two. My work-life balance was perfect and life overall was great, I was happy. What I didn't know was that it was all about to change.

It was the 30th of June and I woke up with another headache. My simple remedy was to take some pain-relieving medication. I never gave it a thought that popping painkillers had become a daily ritual over the previous couple of weeks. I had been experiencing some blurry vision and had made an appointment and visited my eye specialist the previous week. Having had my eyes lasered the previous year I was concerned that I was having some side effects from my eye operation. After extensive testing, he assured me my eyesight was perfect and whatever was causing the blurry vision definitely wasn't my eyes.

My husband at the time, an interstate truck driver, was at home which was unusual, so I left my children with him so I could do my grocery shopping. Whilst out shopping my head started to ache again and the blurry vision was back. It got so bad that I didn't finish my shopping but headed for home. I lived about 7 Kilometers from town. During the trip home I stopped twice to try and wait for my vision to clear. I thought that this must be what a migraine is like. My mother suffered from migraines at times when I was younger and now, I was appreciating how bad they must have been. I made it home and went to bed with the good old tried and tested wet washer on my forehead.

Later that day my sister Kylie came by on her way to my parents' house another 15 minutes out of town. She suggested that as my husband was about to leave, I should go with her to my parents' home where Mum would feed and bath my two children, and then I could come back home, put them straight to bed and not have to worry. I agreed if I didn't have to drive. I arrived at my parents' house and Mum and Kylie took my children inside. I walked in holding my forehead and immediately laid down on the couch saying hello to my Dad on the way in. Within a minute or two of lying on the couch, I felt unusual. I can't quite describe it but I knew it wasn't normal. I got up off the couch, announced to my father that I didn't feel well and then I collapsed. Little did I know I had a stroke! After an unknown timeframe, I became semiconscious and was immediately aware that I could not talk and could not move parts of my body. The next 24 hours were a blur. I had another small secondary stroke the next night. Things were happening around me that I did not understand. What I did realize though was that I was no longer in control.

Until this very moment, I had felt I was in control of everything around me. It now appeared that I was not. My life was, to me, crumbling down around me. My speech was impaired so communication was difficult. I had no mobility down one side of my body and could not function independently. It became apparent that my husband didn't know where my daughter went to daycare and while he knew the school my son went to, he wasn't sure where to drop him or at what times. My normal routine was not known to any of my family or friends in any great detail. It's not that my husband was a bad father; it was the fact that I had structured my life around me as I was the nucleus for the success of my business and life. Once I was removed from it, my life could not function correctly. We had a business to run and children to look after and little did I know at that time, it was going to be a further 12 months before I was capable of returning to 'normal.'

Over the coming months, I had to concentrate on my recovery, I had no choice but to focus on my health. I had to rely greatly on people around me for major support. People around me were doing everything they possibly could without knowing what had to be done. My daily life was usually very busy and there was no way for my support network to know what had to be dealt with until something became evident to them, usually by way of urgency or drama. How they coped I do not know and I am really grateful for their help and support.

During this period, I not only learned how to walk, talk, and feed myself again, I had to discover a whole new way of controlling my life. This event in my life totally transformed the way I live and work. I never wanted my life or my business to be out of control ever again.

My recovery was outstanding; as I improved physically and mentally, I started to put some simple strategies into my life and business. Using simple systems, I wanted to have control even when I wasn't there to be in control. I wanted my family and business to grow and thrive even in turbulent times. Later on, when I opened a new start-up business I realized that I needed it to grow. It could not be in the start-up phase for too long; the younger it was the more vulnerable it would be if I was ever to become incapacitated again.

My systems developed more and more. They were proving to be successful. Time after time my systems helped grow my businesses fast, allowed me to be in control, and never allowed for chaos at home or at work. Soon I had other business owners wanting to know what I was doing. I was asked, "How can you do so much in your day?" "How do you get everything done?" "You seem to be everywhere!" "You must be superwoman!" Well, no, I am not a superwoman but I am self-disciplined at following a few easy steps every day. By doing this, it appears that I achieve the unachievable. I have never had so much time to spend time with family and friends and most importantly spend time with myself. I now have the money to choose when and where I want to eat out for dinner, where and how I travel, and what I want to buy.

The life that I always wanted is now here.

I have used 5 Simple Steps to Freedom and Success in all of the businesses that I have owned and are also used within my coaching client's businesses.

These steps are where I focus my time while running my 9 companies in 45 countries and are allocated to my ideal week.

These 5 Simple Steps to Freedom and Success are:

Database Management

Sometimes in business, this is the only asset you have to really sell. Your chairs, computers, and desks are worthless, to say the least. Imagine if you could say to your potential purchaser I have a database of X amount of people, I have contacted them every month, I have all of their current details, I have their history of what business they have done with me and I have a system in place for repeat business with them which equates to $Y in potential income. Now wouldn't that be worth something to a potential buyer of your business?

Relationship Building

I am always a big advocate of not just getting new clients but building relationships. People buy from people! It is much easier to do business with people you have a relationship with rather than trying to sell something to someone you don't know.

Current Clients

So many people spend hours trying to find new clients and forget about looking after their current clients. These are people who know you, like you, and trust you. It is so much easier to do further business with these people and sell them other products and services you have. More importantly, it is easy to have them refer others to you.

New Clients

As I said previously most businesses actually spend most of their time in this area and forget about looking after their current clients. New clients must have an exceptional experience from day one but also on day 229 and day 1574.

Self-Promotion

I want to say straight up – don't get all shy or embarrassed about promoting yourself. You don't have to be the life of the party to get everyone to know who you are and depending on what type of party it is, this may not position you as the expert in your industry.

If you allocate time for each of these areas and stay consistent and persistent, you and your business will grow beyond belief. Please reach out to me if you have any questions.

SUZIE BOWERS

Six-Figure Business Strategist / Author /
HypnoTherapist

https://www.facebook.com/suzie.bowers

https://www.facebook.com/HypnoProfessional

https://www.instagram.com/hypnoticsuzie

https://www.souldiscoverycoach.com

Since 1995, Suzie Bowers has been helping others to overcome limiting beliefs and achieve success and joy in life through her Soul Discovery Coaching ProgramTM. Suzie opened her private therapy practice, California Hypnosis Center & Academy, in her hometown of Stockton, California.

An entrepreneur at an early age, Suzie achieved many successes in her first career in real estate where she learned the power of a positive mindset, systems, and mentorship in creating a six-figure business. Suzie then transferred that experience to her self-improvement practice where she has helped thousands of clients achieve their personal best.

In 2011, Suzie launched HypnoProfessional Publishing Company, with the sole purpose of educating and supporting industry leaders in creating successful, scalable businesses using her signature Six-Figure Success System.

A sought-out speaker and trainer, Suzie is the author of several books, including Ten Keys to Living a Soul Life, Ways to Quit Smoking, and Suzie Bowers' Six Figure Success System, Where Passion & Purpose Change People's Lives. Coming soon: Dragonfly ~ Journey into Light and Transformation8, 8 Weeks to a New You.

Suzie is successfully teaching other entrepreneurs in the healing fields to expand their impact and grow their thriving businesses worldwide through online systems, best practices, and mentorship.

She is also the host of Everything Hypnosis, Ignite Your Awesomeness, LIVE every Wednesday at 11:11 am Pacific Time, where she interviews successful entrepreneurs worldwide in the self-improvement industry.

Passion, Purpose & Prosperity

By Suzie Bowers

When we think of passion, we often connect sex and love to the idea of it, and certainly, we want that in our intimate relationships. But passion is and can be so much more than that when applied to every area of our lives and businesses to live the most successful and happy life we can imagine for ourselves.

Passion!

What does it mean to be truly passionate? According to the Urban Dictionary:

"Passion is when you put more energy into something than is required to do it. It is more than just enthusiasm or excitement, passion is the ambition that is materialized into action to put as much heart, mind, body, and soul into something as is possible."

What a powerful statement. Passion encompasses all that we are: mentally, physically, emotionally, and spiritually. This is truly how I felt when I discovered the power of the human mind, which includes the unlimited ability to create, heal, and become the best version of myself. I found myself passionate about sharing this with others.

We are all born because of passion. It must take a great deal of physical, sexual emotional, and spiritual energy to be born. Think about the drive and intention of our soul to muster the courage and will to take human form and live on the earth plane.

Beyond that, many particulars had to come together in the perfect combination for us to even be here. In an explosion of atomic energy, cells and chromosomes had to line up in just the right way.

Our very existence is a miracle of focused passion.

That same drive or inspiration to enjoy life is a force of nature and the very purpose of our existence. When we apply passion to our everyday lives and businesses, miracles begin to happen. Intention combined with passion creates a vortex for the manifestation of our most cherished dreams, desires, and reasons for being here. Passion for our work helps us to jump out of bed and do the things necessary to succeed.

By nature, we are passionate beings. The "soul" self, mentioned above in the definition of "passion," can be described as the immortal part of us, our essence, life force, spirit, or divine spark. We would have to be passionate to access enough energy, intention, and force to become and create the life we desire and deserve.

Purpose!

What does it mean when you have a purpose in your life? Have you ever asked yourself, "What the heck is my purpose for being here?"

"Purpose is the reason why something exists or is done, made, or used." (Webster's dictionary.)

Passion and Purpose together are a powerful force for creation.

Your joy, your enthusiasm, and your purpose are the reasons for what you do, and why you are here. If you have passion for something, you're going to put your spirit, your excitement, and your action into it, which is living your life on purpose.

Simply stated: Your purpose is the reason why you're doing it.

Purpose is unique to each of us as we are individual energy beings from the same source of all love and light manifested in human form, enjoying our unique experience.

For example, I have a passion for helping others feel empowered and successful. My passion leads me to my purpose, to be the best business coach and hypnotherapist I can be, and to help others achieve success in their lives.

Prosperity!

What does Prosperity mean to you?

Prosperity can mean a lot of things, like having extra money over what you need to survive. Prosperity can also equal abundance, which can mean different things to each of us.

When we're passionate and we're on our purpose, we set into motion the things that give us joy and love in our life. Prosperity can also mean health, success, fulfillment, creating a business, and the lifestyle freedom that brings us the kind of prosperity and abundance so we can live our life on our purpose and with passion.

Prosperity may mean being able to do the things you want to do when you want to do them. It's different for everyone, yet prosperity is the result of applying passion and purpose to your life and your business.

I invite you to discover what you are passionate about.

How do you know what you are passionate about? How do you know what your purpose is?

Once you figure out what you are passionate about, and what you love, then you will discover your purpose. Passion is what makes you happy, what gets you out of bed in the morning, and what you've always felt inspired to do.

What is it that feeds your soul, your joy, and when you do it, you feel better for it? You feel fulfilled, you're flying, you're soaring, you're radiating happiness. You are in the flow of goodness, in the flow of the universe. This is your purpose.

When I was originally in my real estate career, I discovered the power of being in the flow. I had a great deal of passion for helping people sell their homes or find new homes. When I set my intention to serve others, opportunities and prosperity dropped into my lap. It was seemingly effortless. But there were times when I was efforting.

What is "efforting?"

Efforting is the opposite of being in the flow, you're not in the correct vibration for attraction and creation. I'm speaking about the kind of efforting that is painful, stressful, worrisome, and self-centered. It's about "What's in it for me," instead of, "How may I serve today?" Efforting is a product of fear.

It's not that you don't need to take action to get things done. Often, we have to feel our fears and move through them anyway. The universe loves action, passionate action. Passion and Purpose are the driving forces that keep us moving forward even when obstacles appear.

When you're passionate and on your purpose, you are in service, your energy vibration is high and in the love zone, and this is when prosperity flows to you. When you're efforting, you're pushing your prosperity away.

How can we get into the flow and stop being fearful?

Set your intention for prosperity and joy. Get clear on it. This could be a dollar amount, an experience like a vacation or a trip around the world, time with your family, or it may be the intention to live your life on your terms. For example, not having to be somewhere at 8 a.m. on Monday.

This is my intention because I enjoy quiet, reflective, and creative time on Monday mornings. Not only am I passionate about this, but it is my prosperity!

Your intention could be to connect with and help as many people to achieve their dreams today as possible. Or maybe you want to rescue animals or sell your artwork. When you come from this place of love and passion, purpose-driven, it becomes easy to take the actions that will lead you to success.

Next, set your intention that everything will go exactly as it should in the highest and the best way and at perfect timing for all concerned. Feel the feelings of future gratitude as if you already have what you desire.

Finally, let go! Release any expectations and surrender. Surrender may not be what you think. I'll be the first one to tell you to never, ever give up! Surrender as it pertains to our 3 Ps: Passion, Purpose, Prosperity, are trust and faith that all is well and exactly as it should be, while you make connections from your heart and continue to act toward your purpose.

Everyone is here for a divine purpose that is uniquely theirs. How do you know what that purpose is? You know because you'll feel joyful. When you're living your purpose for being here on Earth, you are happy and fulfilled. It's the simplest thing in the world.

I often wonder why more people don't allow themselves to embrace their passion and live it fully. Then I recall being full of fear to leave the "security" of a job.

Working for someone else sucked the joy right out of me and left me feeling depressed and hopeless. There is no amount of money for me that makes losing my time freedom worth it.

Maybe you are feeling this way. Maybe you are uncertain what would happen if you decided to embrace your passion and live life on your terms.

I love helping others with hypnotherapy, coaching, and building successful businesses. That is my passion and my purpose. My prosperity comes as a result of helping others, and the way I get to live my life every day, working part-time, making an income that allows me to be there for my family and friends, and spending time doing the things I love.

I want this for you too.

DIONNE PHILLIPS

Celebrity Eyelash Extension Expert & Founder

https://www.dlashes.com/

https://www.instagram.com/dlashes

Dionne Phillips has been dubbed the premier authority in celebrity eyelash extensions and faux lashes. She began her career servicing clients such as Victoria Beckham, Naomi Campbell, Renee Zellweger, Lindsay Lohan, Mary J. Blige, and a host of others while working at a well-known, prestigious salon.

After several successful years of providing LA's most beautiful and durable eyelashes, Dionne decided to strike out on her own, launching D'Lashes in 2005.

From Start-Up To Celebrity Expert

Q & A With Dionne Phillips

1) You are known as the "pioneer of eyelash extensions to Hollywood's A-List". Can you tell us some of the celebrities you have worked with?

- Brandy

- Alyssa Milano

- Christina Ricci

- Serena Williams

- Paula Abdul

- Toni Braxton

- Renee Zellweger

2) How did you get started and where?

It started with a vision. I wanted to be around beautiful people. It caught on from word of mouth and I went from one celebrity to another. I was out at events and talking to everyone, everywhere I could.

I started in my apartment. I didn't really realize that I had a business. I would talk to girls at my auditions about putting lashes on them and it took off from there.

3) **What was your approach to staying locked into the business as you grew it?**

I stayed locked in by solving a problem. I knew the women wanted it so I had to challenge myself to make it better day after day. I didn't know what I was doing but I just wanted to stay focused on solving the problem I found.

4) **What motivates you to do what you do?**

I would walk around NYC looking at the tall buildings and I knew something out there was bigger than me. I was focused. I stayed inspired by my client's stories and the lives they were living.

5) **When you were transitioning from a job to a business, what were some of the struggles you had, and did you have a coach or mentor in the early days?**

I was overwhelmed and didn't know what to do. So I had to make processes. Too many people were reaching out via phone call, text email, etc. So I knew I had to tackle one task at a time and keep the clients together while executing my process.

I also never thought about raising funds and started with only $65.

6) You studied in New York for 5 years to perfect your technique. What kept you motivated during that time?

I perfected the technique and all of the details to apply the lashes so well that I could do it in my sleep. I perfected the process before even reaching out for funding. I did my business plan after I started my business so I was able to use actual numbers for the plan. I saved 1/2 of the money from every client.

I was single and living in a studio apartment next to the Lincoln Tunnel in NYC.

7) Who was the first big star that you landed that you couldn't believe?

- Victoria Beckham

- Paris Hilton

8) Can you talk about breaking into the industry as an African American Woman?

I am a pioneer in my industry. It is a challenge at times but I do not allow that to steal my focus. I try to think outside the box when it comes to dealing with the challenges of running a business as a black, female business owner. I have to make sure that I have to do things differently so I can break through the ceiling.

9) What do you enjoy doing when you are not working?

- My passion is working out and drumming.

- I love bass and female drummers.

- I take drum lessons every Sunday.

- I played drums for ….." missing you"

10) What mentors do you have and what entrepreneurs do you look up to?

Barbara Ann Corcoran is an American businesswoman, investor, speaker, consultant, syndicated columnist, author, and television personality. As a television personality, she is a "Shark" investor on ABC's Shark Tank.

Marcus Anthony Lemonis is a Lebanese-born American businessman, investor, television personality, philanthropist, and politician.

BOOK – Awaken the Giant Within: How to Take Immediate Control of Your Mental, Emotional, Physical and Financial Destiny! – Tony Robbins

11) What struggles did you have to overcome en route to building your success?

I have been rejected by banks and people over and over again. I just hustle and saved my own money and made it happen.

When people said "you need a vacation" I would tell them that I will take a trip when I have clients.

I went to school with some well-to-do families and wanted to do better and be better. I wanted to be the "triple threat".

12) Do you have any employees?

I do not. I am in the recruiting phase.

It is a challenge that everyone wants me and just me.

It is a huge goal to hire and train people to do what I do so that I can grow beyond what I can do by myself.

13) What does your husband do now that you have found success?

He works for Callaway Golf company. But when he is in town he likes to help out where he can with the business.

14) What fears and doubts did you battle before starting your business or now even?

Not getting somewhere first was a big fear. I have to tell myself no, I will build my community on my time, and eventually, a buyer will find me.

15) What exactly is your product line?

It is a line of strip lashes that look like eyelash extensions without having to see me in person.

16) What errors did you make along the path to success that slowed down your success?

Yes, there is a certain person that I would have partnered with faster but I wanted to make sure that I did it on my own.

Also, not having enough time to build a solid team because I am too busy inside the business.

17) How many years ago did you start your business?

1998 – 20+ years ago.

18) If you could go back and sit with a younger self what would you say to yourself?

Do it now. Do everything now. Do not wait to perfect the art for long. Just get started.

Don't worry about the technique. If you have a vision of this just do it. Take action now.

19) How do you use your "gut" feeling to make business decisions?

I listen to my gut constantly. I feel as though it is God speaking and guiding. If it doesn't feel right then I will not do it.

I was raised in a Baptist Christian family but wasn't sure what I believed. But as I grew up I found my faith and can't explain it to other people.

My favorite is Bishop Noel Jones.

20) What is the #1 resource that every entrepreneur who is listening needs to read?

- Entrepreneur Magazine

- Inc. Magazine

21) What one thing would you do with your business if you knew you could not fail?

I have an amazing product and idea that I am currently working on.

22) What is a skill, that if you had would double your business?

Microblading – Little 3D hairs that are etched in the eyelashes. I am going to school to learn this technique and it will double my business.

23) If the Wall Street Journal or Forbes were to write a story about you, what would you want it to say?

That I built a business and was the authority in the $4 billion eyelash industry.

24) What is the best coaching and advice you could give to entrepreneurs?

- Number 1 – Do it right now. Whatever vision you have. Do not listen to people when they say you are crazy.

- Number 2 – know your numbers and your process.

ELéONORE DE POSSON

Spiritual Teacher / Healer / Speaker / Published
Author

www.eleonoredeposson.com

www.instagram.com/eledeposson

Eleonore is a Spiritual Teacher, Healer, Published Author, and Host of the Sacred Roots Podcast.

She founded the Sacred Roots Modern Mystery School where she helps women entrepreneurs, feminine leaders, and wayshowers live their purpose, lead in soul alignment and embody their feminine energy so that they can impact more people and experience effortless abundance, ease, and flow.

Embody Your Feminine Energy To Lead With Intuition, Purpose, Money, and Flow

By Eléonore de Posson

Once upon a time, in a Mediterranean country, lived a very independent, strong, intuitive woman who didn't live by any rules, except hers. She was wise, powerful, psychic, gifted, and incredibly beautiful. She knew her power and gifting, but she would only use them to serve those who needed it.

One day, she met a man. And she taught him a lot of sacred practices to increase his power, healing abilities, magnetism, and leadership. They fell deeply in love. Together, they were one. They were unstoppable. They used their incredible talents to heal the world and build something new. With them, there was hope. There was peace. There was love... but also jealousy and competition.

When he died, she was told to leave. The men around her feared her. They were impressed and challenged by her as they did not understand her. She was grieving, tired of being threatened, and chose to leave. And so, the world almost forgot about her.

This story has been shared around fires at night and between closed doors at day. This is the story of Mary Magdalene. Her story but not His-tory, of course. But this is your story too. Because inside of you, lies a wise, powerful, gifted, magnetic woman that has also been threatened and asked to leave because she was too noisy, too weird, too smart, simply too much. A part of you got tired of the threats and criticism and accepted to stay small in order to stay safe.

I am here to call you out. We need that part of you back. The Wise Woman. The Witch. The Whore. The Bitch. The Priestess. The Healer. The Midwife. The Powerful and Gifted Woman. We need her. We need you and your full authenticity. We need your power because you chose it precisely to be expressed during this incarnation. You did not choose to hide it.

I know it's been hard. I know it's been scary. I know you've simply wanted to be loved for who you are but have kept encountering closed doors or jealous brothers and sisters. I did as well. And your mother, grandmothers, and great-grandmothers too. The diminishing of the feminine has been going on for centuries and still is, in a more subtle and virtual way - thank you social media.

I know a part of you is resisting reclaiming your power because it's been scary to be really yourself. Your brain, body, and cells remember. They are imprinted with past lives and transgenerational trauma of being chased, tortured, or killed for being in your power. But you know better now. You know it won't happen again. And you know it is time. The world is moving towards Matriarchy again and women are being called to lead. Yes, you reading these pages, are being called to lead.

So, it is time to be fully yourself.

It is time to speak your truth.

It is time to share your unique gifting with the world.

It is time to smile at those who are telling you that you are too much.

It is time to heal this beautiful planet and create a new one, together.

Let go of what is expected of you.

Let go of doing things the way you *think* they *should* be done.

Let go of strategies that do not make you feel good.

Let go of the hustle because you've been told it was the only way.

Let go of the pressure to be a perfect mother, business owner, wife, friend, best friend.

There is so much that wants to come through you. You were selected and highly qualified to fill in the role of your life. And you are safe to do so as you have a whole Universe, Goddess, Mother Earth - call it the way you like - supporting, serving, and loving you. All you have to do is to step fully into your most authentic self and surrender to the Great Plan of the

Great Goddess. And in exchange for embodying the colors of your Soul, you will be highly rewarded. More than in your wildest dreams.

Are you ready to reclaim your feminine power now?

1) Feminine Energy

We live in a very masculine world. It is all about hustle and burn-out is worn like a badge of honor. *Set goals and strive to reach them. Work hard, Play hard.* But it is keeping us away from our true power. Our Feminine Power moves in flow and aligns us with our soul's purpose. We need masculine energy, for sure. But we mostly need to reclaim our feminine energy so that we can create a Sacred Union between our feminine and masculine, which is key to birthing our unique power and experiencing wealth in all areas of our lives.

Everything starts with the Feminine; every man is born from the womb of a woman. Every day, which is masculine, starts at midnight when it is the night, which is feminine. When your feminine energy is fully embodied and present in your life and business, you slowly unleash 6 gifts inside of you:

2) Authenticity.

You speak your truth, share your gifts and purpose with the world and embrace your femininity. Your work does not feel like work anymore. You create from a place of alignment and pleasure because your genius is expressed through your authenticity.

3) Magnetism.

As you have stepped fully into who you are, "your people" start to recognize you. Your magnetism is activated by your authenticity. And as you slow down and remember that there is nothing to prove, nowhere to be rather than in this present moment, you magnetize more money, opportunities, and love. And you impact hundreds, thousands, and maybe even millions of lives.

4) Intuition

When you move from your feminine energy, you are very tapped in. You know the sound of your intuition and do not confuse it with the stubborn, fear-based, judgmental voice of your ego. You hear your soul when you dance, sing, walk or rest. And you deeply trust that whisper in the wind, as it has never failed you. Especially when it did not make any sense at the moment.

5) Surrender

As you have already activated the gifts of authenticity, magnetism, and intuition, you are now ready to release control and deeply, deeply trust yourself and your co-creator. You surrender. You know you can't see the greater plan. But you know there is one and you know that when you allow uncertainty to overtake your life, then magic is about to happen. You surrender to Life and settle in peace in your body, heart, and soul.

6) Receiving

As women, we know how to give. We are amazingly good at understanding our kids, friends, partners, and clients' needs. But our innate energy is about receiving. By allowing ourselves to receive, we participate in the flow of life that is naturally moving through us. By resisting to receive and deflecting love, compliments, money, or support, we are blocking the natural flow of life, slowly breaking the Law of Exchange, and stopping Life on its course. At this point of reconnecting and embodying your feminine energy, you are ready to reopen your receiving channel and allow Life to flow fully through you. Your creative power is activated and you finally receive all that you have been dreaming of, and much more.

7) Grounding

Finally, your soul is fully embodied and present in your body. You are grounded. Which allows you to be even more intuitive and psychic. Your power is embodied and shines through your whole body and aura.

How to Embody your Divine Feminine

Your journey to wealth in all areas of your life starts here. Together we are going to activate your Gift of Authenticity which holds your power and genius. Grab a journal and pen, put a timer on 30 minutes, and answer the following questions:

Start with saying "no":

- What is currently draining your energy?

- What would you like to say "no" to but haven't done it yet?

- What are you CHOOSING to say "no" to today?

- How will others benefit from this?

Before you can start to say "yes":

- What story / experience / gifts are you afraid of talking about or keeping mostly to yourself?

- What part of yourself are you hiding?

- How could others benefit from hearing that story / receiving your gift / or seeing you fully?

- How would you choose to express yourself and your gifting if you knew you were safe and loved?

- Write down 5 reasons, or 5 facts showing you that you are safe expressing this today.

- Choose to take action.

Now, you can also download my free meditation "Meet Your Divine Feminine" and start connecting energetically with that potent, wise, and gifted part of yourself. She is waiting for you:

www.eleonoredeposson.com/dfmeditation

Enjoy the meditation, take the action you have written down earlier and remember to genuinely express your feminine power to the world. Health, Wealth, Purpose, Joy, and fulfillment are waiting for you on the other side.

AISLING SMITH VANCE

Purpose Coach / Clinical Hypnotherapist /
Counsellor / Master Coach / Trainer of NLP

https://www.instagram.com/aislingsmithvance

https://web.facebook.com/asmithcavan

https://aisling-smith-9d98.mykajabi.com/asv-empowered-women-
book-giveaway

Ash Book Download

As we embark on a post-Covid world, we all understand that our mental health is more important than ever in ensuring we live holistically healthy, happy, and fulfilled lives.

Aisling Smith Vance, (Ash), is a highly accomplished businesswoman, podcaster, and mother. Having built multiple businesses globally, appeared in the reality TV show The Apprentice, and brokered many multi-million dollar business deals, Aisling has discovered the importance of true fulfillment in life, and how to achieve it.

After spending over a decade in the psychological analysis of consumer and human behavior, Aisling decided it was time to turn her gifts and talents into really helping people. Helping people to overcome their innermost fears, anxiety, and blockages. Helping people to perform at the highest level in their lives, relationships, and careers. Helping people to discover their Purpose, become the Best Version of themselves, and Live a Life true to their Beliefs and Aspirations.

As a Clinical Hypnotherapist, Counsellor, Master Coach, and Trainer of NLP, Coaching, and Hypnosis; Ash also runs training courses. For people who wish to learn more about NLP & personal development and pursue a career as a Coach or Therapist in her coaches training company, The Institute of Empowered Psychology. Which Aisling co-owns and runs with the magnificent Fran Harper. Together they create confident coaches and help them develop successful coaches businesses in their niches with their ideal clients.

Aisling is available for Personal Breakthrough Sessions, 1-1 Coaching, and Hypnotherapy Sessions. Contact Ash directly for more information.

Defining YOU! How To Use Your Passion To Discover Your Purpose and Create Prosperity

By Aisling Smith Vance

Mark Twain once said *"The Two most important days in your life are the Day you were Born and the Day you Find out Why"*

Have you ever wondered about those people who were really happy in life? You know, the people who seem to have it all figured out! They have the perfect job, and perfect income and they're happy, wealthy, and fulfilled. Have you ever looked at them and wondered, "how did you create this for yourself?"

At least, I know, I often did. As I flailed around from career to career for 20 years in the pursuit of discovering 'My Purpose', I wondered why it was so difficult to be happy and also, how many people were really happy with what they had chosen to do with their lives?

I mean let's take this back a step, to high school, sometimes, people choose their career upon what their parents want them to be, "we are all doctors, four generations of doctors in our family" or because of a parent's unfulfilled dreams. "I never had the time money or resources to study Law - that's going to be different for my Sandra, she is going to go to Harvard Law and will become a Lawyer". For others who have no idea, it's either whatever they fall into through a recommendation or work experience or based upon a test they undertake in a career guidance class!

My story is that I was a passionate athlete back in high school. I decided that I wanted to be a Physiotherapist, so I pursued that, only to drop out of University after failing Anatomy five times. So there I was a college dropout, my dreams in shreds! My chances of success as a Physiotherapist were fairly slim without a good foundation in Anatomy. When I look back now I know that there were two reasons that I wanted to become a Physiotherapist:

1. To be within close proximity to successful male sports players and

2. To open a chain of Physiotherapy clinics across the country.

Both of these driving forces could have been fulfilled without the need for me to undertake a grueling 5 years in University studying a subject that was not best suited to my aptitudes.

After 20 years of industry hopping. Jumping from Food Service to Sales, Hospitality to Sales to Entrepreneurship, to Hospitality, to Sales to Event Management, to Sales, to TV Production, and back to Sales... I was exhausted and burnt out. Now don't get me wrong, I absolutely loved the path and the trajectory of my career, however, I never completely felt like I had nailed it, that I had found my purpose. Have you ever felt that way?

That was of course until I studied NLP and became a Coach.

So why, you may ask, have I dedicated my life to helping others discover their purpose? Well - that is my passion, my driving force, it's what lights me up inside and allows me to sleep at night feeling truly fulfilled!

The journey to discovering your purpose begins with self-discovery. You must be willing to change anything that is not assisting you in becoming that happy, fulfilled version of yourself. And I had spent 12 years doing that.

The 4 requisites for change are:

1. Make a Decision to Change.

2. Remove Emotional Baggage.

3. Focus on What you Want.

4. Take Action Towards Achieving What you Want.

After spending countless years as an aspiring coach and then as a trainer of NLP and Life Coaching, what I have discovered is that you may have multiple purposes in life and they may vary at stages of your life. But you have to make a decision to go for it.

So I developed a 6 step formula for change which I would like to share with you today - in the hope that this will help you to Discover your Purpose!

(Use the QR code to download the workbook attached to this formula to help)

Ash Book Download

Step 1. The Ultimate Self Discovery Framework

A lot of people are in the wrong place, the wrong career, or the wrong relationship because they don't know who they are. They have never taken the time to discover their true self. It's time to take out the workbook or a journal and answer some questions that will help you in;

1. Being yourself

2. Understanding yourself

3. Appreciating yourself

4. Projecting yourself

And the bonus to this section is the **WHO AM I** formula. This section is so large it warrants its own book - which I have begun to write.

There are many different things that make up "Who YOU Are" like for example, your Values, your Beliefs, your personality, your heritage, your ancestry, and there are many different tests that can help you discover more about yourself, who you are and what your type is good at.

Step 2. Passion - What Lights Me Up

If you don't know what your passion is, it's time to think about it - it's going to be difficult to use it to discover your purpose and create prosperity if you don't! So use the workbook to discover what makes you smile. What you can do without thinking. What is really easy to do that brings you the most joy. If you had all the money in the world, what would you choose to do?

The Keys to Personal Fulfillment:

1.   Connect with your Authenticity

2.   Discover the WHY deep inside

3.   Develop your Self-Belief

Step 3. Breakdown the Blocks

What are the blocks you're experiencing, and what are things that are holding you back from living the life of your dreams? What are your limiting beliefs? If you are in doubt as to what they are or how to find them these are my tips for breaking down those blocks.

*   Learn your Triggers

*   Overcome Negativity

*   Tame your inner voice

*   Knockdown barriers

*   Fuck the begrudgers

Step 4. Understand the 5 P's of Prosperity

Prosperity is not defined merely by wealth and having money, it is about living a rich and fulfilled life. In a developing country, prosperity is having a roof and running water. What does prosperity look like for you? If you can align your life into these 5 P's Prosperity is already yours.

Passionate - having or showing powerful emotions; capable to arouse strong feelings (especially motivating, romantic or sexual)

Purposeful - having purpose; intentional; important; meaningful

Potential - having capability or possibility to happen or succeed; being potent or powerful; expected to be or become

Possibilities - Possible capable of happening, occurring, existing, or being true.

Pleasurable - gratifying; agreeable; abounding in or capable of giving pleasure and satisfaction.

Step 5. Create Infallible Confidence

Confidence is essential to step out of your comfort zone and into the space where the magic happens. If you've lost it, find it. If you've got it, use it! Building confidence is like building muscle at the gym, you have to work on it to maintain it.

Step 6. The Secret to Creating your Life's Purpose

Well now that you've reconnected with yourself, you've discovered your passion, cleared the blocks, developed your confidence, and determined prosperity now uncover what is unique for you.

- What do you do?

- Who do you do it for?

- How do you do it?

Once you 'Discover your Purpose' the Next Steps you take are:

- Write your personal mission statement

- Get a mentor

- Enrol in a course

- Immerse yourself in the subject matter - reading, work experience, Volunteering, immerse yourself in the field.

- Surround yourself with people who have been successful in that field.

I work with people every day to guide them through this formula toward discovering their passion and purpose in life. It saddens me how many people are just plodding through life, unhappy, unsure, unfulfilled - and it doesn't have to be that way.

Studying NLP was the true catalyst for me because it introduced me to the science and theory of how you can be at the effect of your life and have plenty of reasons why you haven't achieved success, happiness, purpose or you can be at cause and have the results of success, happiness, and purpose. It's your choice are you at Cause or Effect.

In and of itself, the purpose of life is to live a life of purpose!

What are the outcomes of discovering your purpose in life?

Happiness, fulfillment, drive, knowingness The even bigger outcome is the more people who are happy and fulfilled in their lives, the more harmony and connection there is in the world. By and large, it is those people who are the ones that we look at that seem to be really happy fulfilled, and have it all figured out.

In closing, I hope that you have found this to be helpful as you strive valiantly toward discovering your Purpose. To help you even more, here are my top 3 tips for taking action:

1. Follow the QR code in my bio to download the workbook to accompany my 6 step formula.

2. You can work with a purpose and empowerment coach like me and work at removing the limiting beliefs, pain, and negative emotions that have held you back so far in your life.

3. You can study NLP, become a coach and utilize your existing skills, experiences, and expertise to help others.

Mahatma Gandhi once said: "The best way to find yourself is to lose yourself in the service of others."

Indeed, finding purpose through coaching is a fulfilling choice that can help you to see that "YOU" are not defined merely by an identity, but in addition by ability, knowledge, passion, love, happiness, sympathy, connection, and solidarity that all together reflect the most essential purpose of human beings – to be virtuous.

FRAN HARPER

Master Trainer in NLP / NLP Coaching / Time Line Therapy and Hypnosis / Motivational & Keynote speaker

https://www.linkedin.com/in/franharper

https://www.facebook.com/me

www.theinstituteofempoweredpsychology.com

35 Years in Business, Specializing in Global Sales & Marketing, Excellence in Communication, Organizational change, Team Building, Performance Excellence, and Mentoring.

Industries include Food Manufacturing, Global Sales, Construction, Wellness, Coaching, and Training.

Master Trainer in NLP, NLP Coaching, Time Line Therapy, and Hypnosis

Motivational & KeyNote speaker

An innovative & unstoppable Director, with a well-formed strategic ability to identify, capitalize and execute on opportunities.

Positive connections are at the forefront of all strategies, together with a no-nonsense approach to business and decision-making to ensure constant progress.

Extremely Proud Mother of Five Accomplished Children.

The No BS Post-Pandemic Guide To Creating The Future You Want!

By Fran Harper

The No BS Post-Pandemic Guide To Creating The Future You Want!

Are you a successful, disillusioned female professional, who's sick of feeling like a doormat every day?

Then you need to take control of your timeline, because, your time and your energy are priceless and irreplaceable!

What's more, no one knows when that time is up, so, we owe it to ourselves to live every day with purpose – our own Purpose!

In August 2020, I was diagnosed with stage 3 colorectal cancer, however, I have 98 years in my timeline, and I have no intention of going anywhere before I'm 98!

I fought, I won and I'm now back stronger than ever...!

Life lessons can be tough, this taught me a lot about what is actually f..ing important, my 5 kids, my beautiful granddaughter, my sisters, my parents, my family, and sharing my message with others.

I learned that traveling the world wasn't the be-all and end-all – or working 18-hour days! Success is so much more than that!

Let me pause right there for a moment …. How many of you have dreams?

Of course, you do, we all do!

How many of us are putting those dreams off until we know what's happening with Covid OR until we get that house we want or until we are thin enough or you know …. whatever it is we tell ourselves?

At some point in life, we are all guilty of not following our dreams and doing what we do because that's what we do! Go figure, that's where our thinking stops!

Who is stopping us from doing anything that we set our minds to?

The actual truth is, we create our own limitations, we create the glass ceilings, then dutifully abide by them, WHY?

We simply relinquish the one thing that sets us apart from all other animals, our power of choice.

This is about taking back that choice and no longer settling for someone else's dreams but really considering what our life could be if we learn to embrace the uncomfortable and create it!

Has it not now been proved by 2 years in lockdown that working from home can be far more productive and efficient!

No more commuting,

Time to get that HIIT class in between Zoom calls.

More time to see the kids, no more having to manage the guilt of leaving the office at 5 pm so you can read that bedtime story for 10 minutes before the kids fall asleep, or you do!

All in the name of creating a balance in life dictated by someone else's dreams and aspirations. Is this what we dreamed of when we were a kid?

Probably not, we wanted to be a Disney princess or a Vet!

For those who haven't achieved that yet, then I wish to open your mind up to the possibility!

Whether a mother, a wife, or a Corporate Power House, everyone has unique skills to offer others?

The truth is ….

If you don't make that choice now, when will the right time be?

Will you just get older and lose your window of opportunity, continue working for people you dislike?

Doing the daily grind?

Feeling uninspired?

Feeling unimportant?

Unfulfilled, lonely, forgotten, past your sell-by date, and lost?

Letting time slip by without truly being accomplished or fulfilled. So how do we change this?

Driving over the bridge towards Melbourne in the early hours of this morning, I had a feeling of total overwhelm, I couldn't place the feeling at first or what had caused the sense of foreboding in me, then it dawned on me, the once humming city was a silhouette, there were no office lights, the city had literally been switched off!

Had this happened so gradually that no one had noticed?

Do you want to be switched off so gradually that you no longer have any drive, passion or motivation?

Melbourne has been widely reported, sadly, as the most locked-down city, when for years, Melbourne was known as the most liveable city!

Melbourne is not alone, if it were, the Great Resignation would not be one of the hottest Blog post topics of 2022!

The time is now to create the awareness and skills needed to never have to go back to any old way of life.

The world is indeed our oyster, for those willing to break out of their comfort zone and take this opportunity! There are no limits!

You owe it to yourself to step into your uniqueness and be the best version of you, that you can be!

Never, have we had the Global opportunity that we now have!

Why would we settle for being told what to do when it is possible and feasible to create our own futures!

What's more, we already have a myriad of skills that are transferrable, making us all unique, and making business simple and accessible. I'm not saying it's easy, but there are proven processes that can be followed to achieve this.

When we decided to explore overseas markets, 10 years were spent traveling around the world creating relationships and building our business. While this may seem glamorous, the novelty wears off after a while and Business lounges at the airport become a functional necessity!

Long periods of time spent alone and away from family, the positive connection will always remain one of my top values, and that no longer means face to face. Those long trips that took 24 hours for a short meeting are a thing of the past!

We are women, we are resourceful and if you follow the Chinese Feng shui', this is the time of the middle-aged women 30-50, so what are you waiting for ....?

The stars are aligning, and you have everything within your grasp, Choice is the Key!

We have been given the gift of disruption, whether the Age of Aquarius means anything to you or not the world is in flux, the time is now to ground yourself, as the world transitions from Earth to air those who take control will ultimately succeed. If you wait for everything to settle down and for your hand to be dealt out for you, you will continue to live a life that is unfulfilled and mediocre and may never realize your full potential. Is that the role model you want to be for future generations?

But, when you open your mind and accept possibility then there are no limits, expansion is a glorious ability to grow and create the future that you truly want.

When you know there is so much more to achieve, and you ask yourself and the Universe the question "How can I ……………?"

You are on the path to self-fulfillment and where that takes you is a unique and spellbinding journey – it may not all be ribbons and unicorns, there may be tears.

Commit to getting out of that comfort zone and seeing what you are capable of – you owe that to yourself, don't you?

So, if you're ready for transformation, we've got you!

My personal development journey started by accident; I was looking for the solution to fix my Global Sales Team, they needed to be able to communicate effectively, only to find out that communication is the response you get, and that I may be part of the problem!

With that pearl of wisdom, I set out to fix it!

My journey unleashed a passion and I trained as a Master Trainer in NLP, Time Line Therapy, and Hypnosis. I embraced my Light and co-founded the Institute of Empowered Psychology to help others do the same.

I may have taken the long road but it gave me life experience, business acumen, and maybe a little wisdom, which now allows me to support clients through their transformations and their business.

The Master Practitioner of Life coaching program incorporates NLP, TLT, and Hypnosis to open our students up to increased awareness, unstoppable confidence, practical skills, and techniques both personally and commercially.

Focussing on internal and external successes, The ACE Club (Aspiring Coach Entrepreneur Club) was created so that you never have to tread this journey alone because it is an end-to-end Self Transformation and Business journey.

Elevating your game and being surrounded and supported by like-minded individuals is a given.

At IEP we motivate you, aimed at restoring your passion, changing your perspective, stopping procrastination, making you feel whole again, and ultimately creating the future that you want, created by you, for you.

Our course not only allows you to focus on what you really want, but it also shows you the steps to get there.

Having trained with so many amazing coaches, the whole Institute is dedicated to building the resourcefulness and Business skills needed to succeed! That's our guarantee!

After this you will be able to… create sustainable 10k months in your coaching business, work from anywhere, work with people that you like, create the opportunity to be a leader, satisfy that you are in charge of your life, enjoy unstoppable confidence and self-esteem, help others easily without selling your soul, make a massive difference, transform your own life and others too.

Your life will shift completely, guaranteed.

So, here's what you do next…

Take a picture of this QR code

Register your email to book a call and receive your New Life planner!

Start your new brilliant life!

I look forward to working with you to create it!

Warm regards

Fran x

JAN HALDANE

Summit Host / International Speaker / Author /
Hypnosis and Coaching Trainer

https://www.facebook.com/janhaldanehypnocoach

https://www.linkedin.com/in/janhaldane/

Jan is a Summit Host, International Speaker, Author, and Hypnosis and Coaching Trainer. Her focus is on training holistic practitioners to help people change their lives through her pre-recorded specialty hypnosis and coaching courses and live hypnosis retreats on Zoom.

She has over 8,000 students in 150 countries.

To reach more people in these times of Covid, Jan hosts virtual summits and her signature podcast The Reclaim Your Life Show based on her bestselling program Hypnorescue: Reclaim Your Life After Narcissistic Abuse. She also teaches others how to create profitable virtual summits and podcasts that enhance their brand and honor their message.

Jan also speaks at international conferences and summits. Her mission is to empower women in their personal and business lives. If you would like Jan to speak at your virtual event or you would like to guest on her podcast, please contact her at jan@janhaldane.com.

Mind Your P's And F's: Mastering The Entrepreneurial Mindset

By Jan Haldane

As a serial entrepreneur for the past 20-something years, I've learned a lot about what gets in the way of having a successful business. You can have all your ducks in a row business-wise but if your mindset is off, it's going to be a long uphill road to profitability. That's because your mindset is everything. It can make or break your business.

On top of this in these times of Covid, is uncertainty. What we thought our business would look like, is often nothing like what it looks like now. For some of us, this is a blessing, but for many, it is a challenge, to say the least.

It was March 12, 2020, as I boarded a Virgin flight to the Gold Coast, Australia. We were on the cusp of Covid in New Zealand and Australia, and the hypnosis conference I was attending was still going ahead. My

2020 schedule was mapped out to include personal travel alongside business travel. A few days on the beach at the Gold Coast, then fly to Sydney to meet a friend and board a 14-day cruise. Life was wonderful, my plan to combine my love of travel, particularly cruising, and speaking at conferences was in place. I was looking forward to speaking in Los Angeles and Toronto later in the year and had a couple of amazing cruises booked. Little did I realize that my life was about to change dramatically.

By the second day at the Gold Coast, countries had begun to advise their citizens to come home while borders were still open. It was crazy trying to get on a flight, but I managed to get home the next day, having to abandon the conference like many others. I nearly kissed the ground when we landed in Auckland. A 2-hour drive saw me home again in the small town where I live.

It soon became apparent that life had changed. New Zealand was locked down quickly, and it was a strict lockdown. What would I do now in my business? How to reach more people when you live in a community of 5,000 people? While all this travel might sound indulgent, I was over 60 and had worked hard and made some big sacrifices to have this lifestyle.

I realized that travel was off the cards for the foreseeable future, online was the place to be and I'd have to come to terms with the technology I'd been avoiding for so long.

I'd always talked about creating online courses, but that was as far as it got because I found the technology daunting. Even worse, everything was video-driven. I had a real thing about appearing on camera. To say it was a steep learning curve would be an understatement. Fast forward a year and I had created a teaching empire completely online. I worked my tail off, to put it mildly.

Here's the thing, I thought it was the lack of tech knowledge that was holding me back in the beginning, when actually it was my mindset. I had to overcome the P's that we discuss in this chapter in order to succeed. Self-awareness is critical to being successful. It's important to drill down to the internal self-talk that's manifesting in our external behaviors.

So, let's look at the four P's first. They are perfectionism, procrastination, paralysis, and people-pleasing. Each one of these relates to an F which is a particular stress response. Think fight, flight, freeze, and fawn.

Paralysis - Have you ever heard the phrase "paralysis by analysis?" Paralysis relates to the freeze stress response. In caveman days we would freeze until the threat had passed. This was fine when actual, physical, saber-tooth tigers were our threat, but not so fine if you're missing opportunities because you are literally frozen and unable to step out of your comfort zone.

Where is this paralysis/freeze coming from?

What is the stress or response?

If you've been turning down opportunities for your business, ask yourself the following questions:

- Is your business the right fit for you?

- Is lack of knowledge of technology scaring you?

- Do you genuinely need more training?

- Are you working with someone, or in an environment, that drains your energy?

- Do many of your clients' issues trigger your own trauma?

Take some time to honestly work through these questions. You won't have a successful business stuck in paralysis/freeze. What would it take to feel motivated about your business again?

Procrastination - Unlike freeze where we actually do nothing, we appear to be working towards our goals when we procrastinate. It's a bit like treading water in the pool instead of swimming the lap to the other end. We're in the water, but we're not progressing. Procrastination is related to the flight stress response. Often, we are very busy doing 'things.' We are lost in our busyness which conceals the fact that we are not achieving anything because we are not taking real action towards a revenue-generating goal for our business. There's a big difference between creating and launching Facebook ads and mindlessly scrolling through Facebook. As an entrepreneur, it's very easy to get distracted by the next shiny object. This could be a new project, tech solution, or social media platform. Each shining new object seems better than the last, but often they are just distractions. Lots of things get started but never get finished. Hence, no more revenue results from all these new things. Your brain is fried and you're heading for exhaustion and burnout. So, what's really going on in your head? Is it an underlying fear of success? Or is it something else?

Perfectionism - Human beings are imperfectly perfect. Perfectionism masks the fear of making mistakes and of course the fear of failure. The 'fight' stress response is related to perfectionism. The problem is often we are fighting ourselves and not a lot gets done because to be less than perfect would not be acceptable to ourselves.

Needing everything to be perfect sets up impossible and unhealthy standards that can lead to anxiety and even physical issues. In some ways, perfectionism is a mask.

- What is it concealing?

- Is there pain and trauma from adverse experiences that continue to hold you back?

- Who dictated in your childhood that everything you did had to be perfect?

Perfectionism is fear-based, consequently creating control freaks. The need to control is of course based on the fear of being out of control.

- How good are you at delegating aspects of your business to others?

- Are you limiting the growth potential of your business by trying to handle everything yourself, even when it's out of your skillset?

Take some time to consider the answers to these questions and reflect on how the answers affect your business.

People Pleasing - Most people have heard of the fight, flight, freeze response. A new addition to this, and the 4th F, is fawn. Of course, fawning or trying to be liked, wouldn't have worked with a saber-tooth tiger but it can save your life in the modern world. It can be a key reason why so many entrepreneurs struggle with success. This is especially true of women. Fawn is a learned stress response often triggered by Complex PTSD. This is the way many women survive in abusive relationships or through traumatic childhoods. By over-giving, always saying yes, and virtually doing anything to be liked. It's also the fuel for a negative money mindset leading to undercharging and/or excessive discounting.

Entrepreneurs running the fawn response find it hard to set boundaries and may be taken advantage of by their clients, leaving a feeling of resentment due to their inability to maintain boundaries around time and money. This is particularly true for those of us drawn to the helping and healing professions who often put others before ourselves to the detriment of our health and well-being. This certainly has its place, but not in business, as compassion fatigue and burnout are real issues that negatively impact your business and your ability to give your best to your clients. Perhaps fawn was a response you learned that ensured your survival with certain people, places, and situations? That's very understandable, but ultimately, it doesn't work well for your business. What boundaries around services, time, and money can you reasonably set and consistently reinforce?

Often, what we learned in our young years as a way to survive is now less than helpful. It got us through when we needed it, but now we want to thrive both personally and professionally. Take some time to answer the questions in this chapter. Really think about whether you're holding on to old stuff that's secretly sabotaging your business success. We entrepreneurs simply don't have the time to stand in our own way. I want to see you succeed and would love to hear your success stories. I'm also available for mindset mentoring.

LAURA LEE KENNY

Wealth Mindset Creator

https://www.facebook.com/lauralee.kenny/

www.LauraLeeKenny.com

Born at the end of the Baby Boomer era in rural New Brunswick, Canada. We had a very large family of 12 children, and as you can imagine, my parents struggled for many years to feed and clothe us. In fact, I started working for other people when I was 12 years old. I became the youngest cosmetic director at age 15 while attending high school, working in the school cafeteria at lunch hour and working in a bakery most evenings and weekends.

Definitely had a blast with Finelle Cosmetics for 25 years and then transferred into investments. Working as Certified Financial Planner for the past 24 years, where I guide clients to reach their financial goals and get ready for retirement. I have been blessed to coach many people with their investments and protection products to live a secure future. Teaching financial literacy and I'll tell you, that we all need to know about this. Let me show you how to easily up-level your income bracket. There are so many ways to earn money and save on taxation while achieving your goals and dreams.

When we start taking care of our money at a young age, it is so easy to guide people to become millionaires. Even the average wage earner can easily become wealthy if they have the desire to change their mindset and implement easy strategies. One of the most important things I have learned about having a wealthy mindset is that we must work on improving our self-image first! Healing and rewiring our mindset will make all the difference in successfully achieving our dreams and goals.

I have been blessed to learn from some great mentors during my journey.

While taking all these programs for my own journey to heal and learn, I now have a calling to share and serve on a greater level. I have been blessed to be a member of Mindvalley's platform. This was where I was introduced to Marissa Peer and studied directly with her and achieved certification as a Rapid Transformational hypnosis coach in Dec 2016. I've completed year One Foundation training with Donna Eden Energy Method in Jan 2019.

Learning to move your energy when you feel blocked is a valuable technique to know.

Started working with Christy Whitman, my Law of Attraction mentor in Feb 2021, and she has helped me align and heal many areas. Also, blessed to be mentored by Peggy McColl, and now a Destiny Coach with her wonderful platform and making Quantum leaps.

Plus, so blessed to have Forbes Riley as my pitch mentor.

So, if you are ready to make Quantum leaps of your own and up-level your life, click the link below and begin saying Yes to yourself. Website: www.LauraLeeKenny.com

What's It Like To Grow Up On The Wrong Side Of The Tracks?
...And how to take Quantum Leaps to get to the other side.

By Laura Lee Kenny

Let me ask you, "*What would you really Love in your Life*"?

This sounds like a simple question but were you able to quickly answer this with confidence and state your secret dreams and desires as an adult.

Now, I admit I grew up in a household that had to make do with very little. Born in a small town in New Brunswick, Canada at the tail end of the baby boom. Being the third child of a dozen healthy children. I knew what it was like to grow up with the bare necessities for many years.

My parents built a very small bungalow house with a kitchen, living room, and 2 bedrooms when they moved in with only 2 small children. No running water inside the house. When we were multiplied to 8 kids we were stacked like sardines in a can. The house doubled in size when the 9th child arrived. Hard to imagine nowadays having 12 kids, with 4 bedrooms and one washroom. We were moving up.

One of my most vivid memories was the excitement I felt when we got a new outfit for the first day of school. I mean jumping up and down excitedly with a big toothpaste smile. It didn't matter that you wore the same outfit for a whole week at a time. New mind if it got a little dirty. Never mind that most of our clothes were wrinkled because most everything was made of 100% cotton in those days. And yes, we were teased about that also.

Christmas was simple. Santa would bring a small stocking with a barley toy and some chicken bones (hard candies), an orange, and some nuts. I always remember getting one gift each from Santa. Usually, clothes when I so wanted a doll or a toy. I later found out that it used to take mom all year to pay off the Stedman's Variety bill for the Xmas gifts. No credit cards back then. And no, we were not the Walton's, like the TV show. "Sparing the rod and spoiling the child", a biblical scripture, was not a worry in our house. And when you went to school, the thick, black leather strap and wooden rulers were a daily discipline for many students. I'm happy to say, somehow, I avoided the strap at school.

So, what's my point here? When you grow up in an environment of lack, it is a real challenge to ever learn how to feel like you have any value. And if you don't feel valuable, how can you ever put yourself first?

I'm not alone here. My story is the story of many others who grew up at this time. Even now, in this land of plenty, there are many who have so little. There are many who do not feel valued and those who have learned to put themselves second and everyone and everything else, First! I only remember hearing that you must work hard, very hard for your money. Money doesn't grow on trees, was one of my mom's favorite sayings. Many of us could fill a page with old negative money beliefs from when we were children.

My Grammy, being a very religious person, told me that the bible says, "It is easier for a camel to go through the eye of a needle than for a rich man to get into the kingdom of God". So, I learned that it was better to be poor and go to heaven someday than to be rich and go to hell. My only 2 choices. What a dilemma, when you are 5 years old, and you think she is talking about a sewing needle. No wonder we pick up limiting beliefs when we are young. Perception is everything! I was in my 50's when I found out the difference. Grammy loved me and she meant well.

Now, you know a little more about me. And deciding to get married very young and have 2 children by age 21, didn't help my chances of breaking the chains of poverty. However, it was still possible. Thank heavens, we made some sound choices with very little knowledge. My Grammy also told me that getting a good education was the way out of poverty". "Study hard and listen to your teachers," was her sage advice. I believe that some of our best teachers do not work in the school system.

Now I worked part-time for most of those years and raised the children. I made very little money but had a lot of fun with the ladies, went on many fabulous trips, and won prizes from a cosmetic company for 25 years. It wasn't just selling lipstick as many people thought. These were great evenings, making women feel and look their best. A novel idea of self-care we must continue to support ourselves...

Let me share how my life has changed. When my youngest graduated high school, I decided to go back to school at age 39. Some might say I was having a mid-life crisis. I was about to embark on a serious career as a financial advisor and I wanted to specialize in retirement planning. That interested me, as we had very little money and I had no retirement plan. It fascinated me that I could show young clients how to become a millionaire so easily when you take action at an early age. And what to do if they started later in life. I worked and studied very hard, with long hours, and being in a male-dominated profession. And to my surprise, my eyes were opened to a different level and type of education that I didn't expect.

Serious goal setting and accountability to someone else were a must, being self-employed.

Who were these people called Napoleon Hill, Bob Proctor, Jim Rohn, Earl Nightingale, and many more and why were they making us set personal goals? Work goals, I understood. Every conference I attended had a motivational speaker. What a great job they had, I thought. And I was hooked on self-development.

Then I got serious in 2016 and got specialized training, to learn how our mind works. What a fascinating subject. I wanted to know why I made some crazy and reckless choices sometimes. Can anyone relate? Have all your decisions worked out for you? While other choices we so easy to make and turned out so well with fabulous results.

So, are you in a Wealthy and Abundance mindset?

Or, do you have a Lack and Poverty Mindset?

I didn't even know what this meant when I first heard these questions.

You are either in one or another, just not at the same time.

Picture a teeter-totter, how two kids take turns making it go up and down.

How do you think you would know what is going on inside your mind?

"By your Results in Health, Wealth, and Happiness", stated Bob Proctor during many of his stickman training demos.

So, are you thriving and living a lifestyle you desire, or are you feeling like you'll never get ahead with your endless bills, on the hamster wheel to nowhere? Living paycheck to paycheck and nothing put away for emergencies, let alone for retirement.

Here are 5 Secret Keys to unlocking keys to Abundance:

1. Learn to Love yourself and heal your heart. Take care of yourself first. Get your mind in alignment in order to accept and receive abundance. This was a tall order for someone who didn't even accept compliments easily.

2. Learn the Laws of the Universe. Law of attraction, what's that all about? You won't go to jail if you break these laws, but you won't pass go and collect money.

3. Watch your words and how you talk to yourself and others is very important. Do you know how to make Quantum leaps on our emotional scale? The feeling is the Secret!

4. Being Focused on your Goals and being disciplined in your actions on a daily basis.

5. There are 2 very important things you need to know about working on your goals, according to many earlier teachers. Bob Proctor continually explained this in his lectures: 1. Where you are.

2. Where you want to go.

So yes, I grew up on the wrong side of the abundance tracks.

It's not about my past!

It is about what I do with my present!

So, I bought my own silver spoon and I found my pot of Gold.

How would you love to be the director, producer, and shining star in your own blockbuster movie? It is my pleasure to share how you can rewrite your own script. One of my favorite tools to use. We use many tools and procedures to easily switch from our old limiting beliefs. What will it cost you to stay in the same place as you are?

Here is an important truth. No one can help you unless you are willing to help yourself. You have to make a committed decision to make changes.

The answers are already inside of you. Let me show you how to up-level your life. You just need a coach to guide you. So, if you're ready to make a Quantum shift, click the links below and start saying yes to your new life.

Website: www.LauraLeeKenny.com

Look for the link Ask for the Gold, for a free hypnosis wealth rewiring recording.

Check out my free resources section.

Many blessings and gratitude, Laura Lee.

JENNIFER C. KANE, D.C.

Chiropractic Physician / Acupuncture Practitioner / Certified Professional Hypnotist / Certified Health Coach

https://www.facebook.com/drjenniferkane

www.drjenniferkane.com

Dr. Jennifer Kane is a Chiropractic Physician and Acupuncture Practitioner, Certified Professional Hypnotist, Certified Health Coach, and an expert in helping people transform their health. Since 2001, Dr. Kane has helped thousands of patients overcome their health challenges and implement physical, mental, and emotional strategies that lead to positive change.

Dr. Kane is an entrepreneur who has owned and operated a successful chiropractic and acupuncture practice for almost 20 years. She was a Clinician at Logan University for ten years and currently teaches acupuncture at Logan University as an Adjunct Faculty Member.

When Dr. Kane was diagnosed with colorectal cancer in 2012, she applied her extensive knowledge of holistic medicine. In addition to traditional cancer care, she used a mind, body, and spirit approach to heal and thrive. Her results were tremendous and far exceeded her doctors' expectations.

From her work with patients and her experience with cancer, Dr. Kane realized the profound impact stress has on health and the vital importance of making lifestyle changes that support a healthy life. She became a Certified Hypnotist to better address the impact of the mind and emotions on healing, and to help people accelerate changes through hypnosis, both in-person and online.

Dr. Kane is passionate about motivating people to change and empowering them to get healthy and stay healthy. She has been a guest speaker at numerous businesses, charities, and international conferences.

If you want Dr. Kane to be the motivational speaker at your next event, visit www.drjenniferkane.com

Creating Calm In The Storm Of Stress

By Jennifer C. Kane, D.C.

As a woman in business, you know how to handle stress. From the everyday stress of life to the unexpected stressors that inevitably occur as you navigate work and life – you have spurred yourself on to higher achievements by learning to channel the energy from stress into greater productivity.

But people can only handle so much stress for so long – until they can't. Everyone responds to stress differently at that tipping point, somewhere along the continuum of 'fight, flight, or freeze.' When the pressure becomes overwhelming – or when life throws you a major curveball – do you respond by feeling angry, anxious, unfocused, or exhausted? Or are you able to create calm in the storm of stress?

The initial response in those first moments of stress can set the tone for the entire experience that follows. When I first heard the life-changing words, "you have cancer," I was shocked by a new reality. But as the big scary story of "what if?" threatened to invade my thoughts, I did the most powerful thing possible. I breathed.

I continued reminding myself to "just breathe," pulling my focus to this moment, NOW. "Just breathe."

In the most stressful moment of my life, this response occurred by grace. Though mindfulness was a skill I had learned in my youth, I had forgotten I had this skill in the stressful years leading up to my cancer diagnosis. But I used it when I needed it most.

To say a cancer diagnosis is stressful is an understatement. To say that cancer treatment is stressful is also an understatement. Intense pain, sleepless nights, hospitals, procedures, waiting for results, and even work provided ample opportunities to build upon my ability to calm myself.

Throughout cancer treatment, I honed this ability to create calm quickly. In addition to deep breathing and reminding myself to "just breathe," I did acupressure to help with pain or anxiety. I guided my mind to peaceful places I had been or to places I had imagined. I moved my body or changed my posture and gently smiled to induce relaxation.

I cannot imagine how I would have gotten through the potentially overwhelming stress of cancer without creating this way of automatically calming stress – its physical manifestation and the thoughts and feelings I was experiencing.

While studying hypnosis years later, I realized I had been hypnotizing myself throughout cancer treatment. Now, these skills are the cornerstone of what I teach my clients so they can transform their stress quickly and easily.

When stress seems overwhelming, we often project ourselves into a scary future. We forget we have successfully overcome stressful situations before. We forget we already have the resources to handle this. We fail to realize this can be the moment to seize control – of our thoughts, emotions, and actions – and create calm in the storm of stress.

In stressful moments, you need a process that works NOW, and it needs to work fast. While sitting in a stressful meeting or waiting to give your presentation, you cannot jog or meditate for 30 minutes to relieve stress. You require something simple, effective, and quick.

It's time to 'X the STRESS.'

For years, I have empowered women in business whose stress has become overwhelming. Once you have learned this process, it can be effective in as little as 30 seconds, though you can spend longer if you have time.

While fast and effective at the moment, the key to your success with 'X the STRESS' is to create an automatic response while you are already calm. Although you can simply follow the steps in 'X the STRESS,' it requires repetition to become automatic. We can easily accomplish this through hypnosis, and I am constantly amazed by the profound changes women make to their response to stress in just one hypnosis session.

Before we begin hypnosis, I ask my clients how they respond to stress. "What do you do when you're stressed?" "What thoughts are you thinking?" "How do you feel?" I watch their breathing become shallow, their expression change, and their muscles tighten as they answer.

We do not spend much time discussing the problem. Instead, we move to solutions. I ask, "In stressful moments, what do you want to do?" "What do you want to think?" "What do you want to feel?" As they imagine the possibilities, their breathing deepens. The stress lines soften. Muscles begin to relax. The more they focus on what they want, the calmer they become.

Since stress often seems overwhelming when the only option is to remain still, most women I work with decide the best action is to breathe consciously. They want to think thoughts like, "I'm okay," or "I'm in control." They want to feel calm.

With this result in mind, we choose 'X.' This is the key to the process of 'X the STRESS.' 'X' is the anchor you choose as a stimulus to immediately connect you to your desired mental and emotional state.

Though an anchor can be a word, color, item, gesture – almost anything – I recommend choosing an anchor that uses your sense of touch. Bringing the thumb and a finger together is an excellent anchor. Acupressure points are also powerful anchors, drawing on thousands of years of success in calming anxiety and stress. Whatever anchor you choose should feel good and be easy to do.

After my clients choose their anchor, I guide them into a deep state of calm through hypnosis. We create a strong association between their anchor and this feeling of calm. We repeatedly practice anchoring this state of calm, strengthening the association until it is automatic and feels natural.

With the anchor firmly established, we create an association between the anchor and the remaining steps in 'X the STRESS.' We repeatedly practice so that every time you use your anchor, it automatically triggers the entire step-by-step sequence of 'X the STRESS.'

Using your anchor will tie everything together, so you can quickly and easily think what you want to think, feel what you want to feel, and do what you want to do to transform this stress.

X the STRESS

X – X is the anchor that you chose.

the

S – Stop and notice the stress. Becoming aware is a powerful step.

T – Take a deep breath. Then let it go – all the way. If it helps, ground yourself in the present moment by noticing the air coming into your nose or focusing on something you see or hear. Allow yourself to be present.

R – Remind yourself to "just breathe" or "calm" or whatever simple word or phrase soothes you.

E – Evoke the feeling you want to feel. Many of my hypnosis clients imagine the calm they feel as they look at the ocean and hear waves lap at the shore. Others remember wandering through a forest or enjoying time with loved ones.

S – Strike a pose. Physical stress can lead to emotional and mental stress. Slumped shoulders increase tension and prevent full diaphragmatic breathing. Modify your posture by aligning your ears, shoulders, and hips. Drop your shoulders away from your ears. Notice how easily your breathing expands. With your expansive breath, your thoughts expand as well.

S – Smile. Not a big, fake smile. You are moving out of stress, not becoming more stressed because you are not feeling happy enough. Think of the Mona Lisa smile or your smile as you relax on the beach. Gently close your mouth and turn your lips up softly, relaxing your facial muscles and inviting relaxation.

Anchors strengthen with intensity and repetition. In hypnosis, we can create an intense state of calm and practice anchoring repeatedly so that 'X the STRESS' becomes automatic. We also practice responding to stressful events calmly as we 'X the STRESS.'

When hypnosis ends, I see a woman who is calm. She looks at me with that strength and certainty that not only can she handle the inevitable stress that is part of work and life, but she can do so with confidence.

Now when we discuss the potential challenges she may face over the days, weeks, and months that will follow, I see a woman who is empowered. She knows she will rise to any challenge. She has already seen herself do just that during hypnosis.

Within days of the session, women tell me they felt calm before and during their big meetings or presentations. They finished that project. They asked for a raise. They say it felt natural to 'X the STRESS' and create calm – as if they had done this before.

Knowing how to 'X the STRESS' impacts far more than the moment of stress. It affects the days leading up to anticipated events, sleep, health, interactions with loved ones, responses to unexpected circumstances, and so much more. It is empowering to know that you can create calm in the storm of any stress.

Visit www.drjenniferkane.com to discover acupressure points to anchor and to download free tools to 'X the STRESS.'

JONI JOHNSTON NEIDIGH

https://jonineidighhypnosis.com/

https://mycommunitybehavioralservices.com/

http://goldmedalmentaltoughness.com/

Joni Johnston Neidigh is a Licensed Mental Health Counselor and has been in private practice for over 30 years. Joni is also a certified clinical hypnotist and trainer for the International Certification Board for Coaches and Hypnotists. She assists people with a myriad of issues including sleep, relaxation, weight loss, smoking cessation, anxiety, fear of flying, confidence, focus, and more.

In addition to her general practice, Joni specializes in athletic performance. She has helped develop athletes from age groups to Olympians and professionals. Joni works with athletes and coaches in a variety of sports including swimming, running, volleyball, soccer, ice hockey, cheerleading, gymnastics, rowing, and golf. Joni has served as a mindset coach on-site at the United States Olympic Swim Trials in 2012, 2016, and 2021. She has also hosted and worked with coaches and teams from other countries as well including Spain, Japan, Brazil, Australia, Scotland, and Italy.

Joni is a public speaker and travels regularly to present to international conferences, clubs, coaches clinics, and colleges. She has served as the main stage speaker for Genentech and Soccerex Miami. The techniques that she teaches can be applied immediately to improve attentional focus, reduce anxiety, and increase motivation.

Joni is the author of the AIM Gold Medal Mental Toughness Success Guide for Athletes as well as the Anger and Violence Intervention Program Success Guide. She offers sports hypnosis training and certification for her Gold Medal Mental Toughness for Hypnotists program. She has produced over 50 audio products to help with general wellness and athletic performance. To learn more about Joni, her products, and her sports hypnosis certification opportunities visit aim-store.net or goldmedalmentaltoughness/training.

To see more of her work visit Jonineidighhypnosis.com.

Gold Medal Inner Coaching: From Fear To Fabulous

By Joni Johnston Neidigh

I can remember those five minutes of fear vividly as I stood there in my middle school cheerleading uniform at the front of my biology class with all eyes on me. My teacher, who also happened to be the football coach, was about to evaluate my presentation. He was a tall, fit, strong man whose presence and loud voice communicated authority. This was my first ever solo presentation and I felt anxious about it from the time the requirement was announced a month earlier. At that time in my life, I was a good student and I was very social and active in school activities. I was a co-head cheerleader and I loved performing and cheering at the athletic events... As far as cheering, I loved the bright lights, the music, and the energy and I looked forward to every opportunity to lead and perform with my teammates. I was optimistic, happy, and generally confident. Life was pretty great especially given that I was in middle school until it wasn't. The day I had dreaded for a month had arrived and when my biology teacher loudly announced that it was my turn to present, I felt startled and overwhelmed with anxiety. My nervous system was on full alert and I could feel the energy from the top of my head to the bottom of my feet. My mind began going through a running list of the "what if's". It sounded like this - What if I can't remember my speech? What if I make a mistake or lose my place? What if I drop my notes? What if people laugh at me? What if I'm embarrassed? What if I'm boring? What if I get a bad grade? It was in this heightened state of anxiety and fear that I began to speak. I remember my voice and my body shaking, my voice cracking, my heart beating fast, my negative self-defeating self-talk playing over and over again, losing my place in the presentation, and just when I thought things couldn't get worse, my teacher yelled loudly "STOP" from the back of the room. He then proceeded to shout "JOHNSTON", my maiden name. He continued "you can get out there in a stadium and cheer for other people, but you can't stand up here and present your outstanding project to your peers. Now start over and this time stop being so selfish thinking about how you look or sound and share your wonderful knowledge with this class. Take a few moments to collect yourself.

As you can imagine, not only had the nightmare of making mistakes and being embarrassed come true but it was amplified by the teacher/coach yelling at me and lecturing me in front of my peers. The emotion I felt inside now was anger at myself and at him and although it did fuel me to finish the presentation it also resulted in intense mental and physical exhaustion. In the days that followed, each and every time I reflected upon the experience I contributed to a life script that resulted in avoidance of any type of solo presentation of any kind when possible. I deeply believed that I wasn't "cut out" for this and that I would never be able to enjoy delivering solo public performances. Most importantly, I had developed an inner coach that would remind me of who I could not be and one who constantly reminded me to say no and avoid any opportunity at any cost.

Continuing to live with this type of inner coach certainly had its consequences. I declined solos in my choir and a chorus that I loved, I believed I wasn't good enough to cheer in high school, I experienced trauma when required to speak in college, and turned down numerous opportunities during the first part of my career as a psychotherapist. Part of me really wanted to do these things, but part of me understood that avoiding the fear and protecting myself was most important. Consciously, I wanted to speak to teams, groups, corporations, and large events. I wanted to feel excited, confident, and motivated to say yes. I wanted to communicate my messages and ideas and reach more people and yet, subconsciously this old way of thinking that began decades ago stemming from a traumatic event was the inner coach running my life, my choices. This inner coach called up a fear response every time danger (public performance) was recognized.

What I eventually learned was that this fear response was just my brain not me, not who I was or who I had to be. As I learned more about the brain and how habits are formed and changed, I began to understand that I could be free of this problem and that I could help my clients become free of many of their problems, too. I added visualization, self-hypnosis, hypnotherapy, and neuro-linguistic programming skills to the tools I was already using in psychotherapy and in my work as a mindset coach with athletes. Most importantly, I began to use what I call my Gold Medal Inner Coaching approach to help people fire an old self-defeating inner coach and hire and develop a great inner coach. This new inner coach is proactive when possible, has the awareness and techniques to shift thoughts when necessary, turns trauma into greater awareness, lessons, and surviving strength, and uses the skill of confidence to say yes to opportunities – consciously and subconsciously.

So, how does this process of developing a great inner coach work? In order to fire your old inner coach and hire a great inner coach, you must give yourself a RAISE. This acronym will help you to remember and check in with yourself to see if you are moving forward. The "R" stands for resetting and shifting. It's important to interrupt old hurtful ways of thinking and reset your thinking to something that will help you. In order to do this, you need the "A" which stands for awareness. This requires taking the time to pay attention to your own thoughts and feelings in a meaningful way. Journaling or jotting down what you notice is a great first step. Self-awareness is the key to change. Next, it's important to address the "I" which represents self-Interest. Ask yourself the question "what are some of the things that I do that represent self-interest?" Take notice or inventory as to whether or not you are doing this. Allow your creative mind to come up with ways, simple or detailed, that you can use to satisfy this need each day. I mentioned self-monitoring your thoughts and jotting them down. The "S" represents your self-talk and when you monitor them and jot them down you can begin to discover your personal patterns of distorted thinking that often lie behind moods that are holding you back. Finally,

It's important to develop a personal elevator speech for yourself. One that is designed about you and for you. A simple way to do this is to write several words or sentences about yourself that you understand to be true about who you are as a person, some of your qualities, your talents, skills, and your interests. By doing this and accepting it as a work in progress you will achieve or maintain your confidence and heightened awareness. You remind yourself of the truth of who you are and what you can do in order to counter any negative evaluations or thoughts you may have in response to various situations. Situations change but your understanding of who you are does not have to change with those situations.

These are just some tips to help you get started to develop a Gold Medal Inner Coach.

You coach yourself 24 hours a day 7 days a week consciously and subconsciously. It's important that you are happy with the person that you are choosing for the job so you may want to consider giving yourself that RAISE.

Reflecting on that day in class that I described earlier, I now own this story in a way that has helped me move forward. I teach other people how to overcome fears that may be holding them back from using their talents, achieving their goals, or doing something they really want to enjoy. I have presented to groups ranging from 60 to 60,000 at international conferences, mental health organizations, corporations, colleges, high schools, athletic teams, dental offices, and hospitals, and with the help of my great inner coach I have moved from fear to fabulous!

To access your great inner coach, go to jonineidighhypnosis.com/inner-coach.

MARTINA KWAN

Champion Mindset / Confidence and Business Coach

@martinakwan

https://www.martinakwan.com/

Born in Hong Kong to a German mother and Chinese father, Martina Kwan was destined for a life that was different. She spent her childhood in Asia, the Middle East, and Europe, but credits living in war-torn Beirut, Lebanon between the ages of 8 and 10, as an experience that defined much of her fearlessness today.

Her unique path in life has shaped her into a woman of drive and determination. Her 2 Master of Science degrees secured her senior roles with KPMG, PwC, Lehman Brothers, and Ian Schrager Hotels. At heart, she is an award-winning Business Entrepreneur and has won 2 Emmy Awards, 4 Telly Awards, and 9 Furniture Design Awards.

Daring to be different is what drives Martina today…literally! 6 years ago, at the age of 50, Martina changed her life completely and was determined to become a race car driver. She is now a 3x Champion, FIA Licensed, and drove professionally in the GT World Challenge America. She co-founded DK Racing School, the World's first school founded by both male and female FIA Licensed race car drivers.

She is also a proud Mother of 2 Teenage girls, a Champion Mindset, Confidence, and Business Coach whose private clients are primarily high-level Female Executives. She also hosts her Signature "She Believed She Could So She Did" and "Xtreme Confidence Mastermind" Women's Retreats at beautiful locations across the Southwest US, which are meant to turn challenges into new beginnings. One of her life's missions now is to inspire women to believe in themselves. Anything is possible, at any age!

How I Survived My Fears From Living Through War And Went On To Succeed In Life

By Martina Kwan

When I was 8 years old, my family decided we would move from my Father's hometown of Hong Kong to my Step Father's hometown of Beirut, Lebanon. Beirut at the time was known as the Paris of the Middle East and at first, it was wonderful spending time at the beach clubs located by the azure blue glistening Mediterranean Sea set against a backdrop of beautiful mountains. The Lebanese war started soon after we moved there and the surrounding neighborhoods became some of the strongholds of the fighters.

The Holiday Inn Beirut, located 2 miles from our apartment building, became a strategic military asset and the frontline of the war. From

October 1975 to March 1976, this hotel became part of an epic battle known as the War of the Hotels in which 25,000 fighters mobilized in our neighborhood, and every night, the warfare continued.

Actually, during the day, when the war started, we were no longer able to go to the Deutsche Schule Beirut. So having no school was kind of fun for my older sister Veronika and me… we became great tree climbers and roller skaters, and would happily go skate down the street from our apartment to pick up our daily homework from the German Embassy. One of our other favorite activities was to collect empty bullet shells and bomb shrapnel from the parking lot next to our apartment.

But things changed when it got dark and the day turned into night.

I would wake up hearing the distinctive sound of machine guns far away, and getting closer and closer to our apartment on Bliss Street. My sister Veronika was my lifeline, I don't think I could have survived without her. My nightly ritual when I heard the machine guns, was to crawl out of my bed and climb into my sister's bed for comfort, and together we would wait to hear the nightly Air Raid Sirens. It was actually not so many planes flying overhead, but groups of fighters on flatbed trucks driving by our buildings shooting off gunfire and rockets.

Our apartment was on the ground floor, and so, in a sense, we used our apartment corridor as our bomb shelter. All of our neighbors from the higher floors would come down and we would sit huddled on each side of our long interior corridor. The thing about the weapons used in Lebanon is that a lot were handmade, AND were far more unpredictable in their action and direction. Do you know how your neighbor shoots off a rocket and it goes sideways instead of in a straight trajectory?? Well, this is kind of like how it was with the real rockets.

So in reality, the exact moment you hear a rocket or bomb being fired is when your body tenses with fear the most…because you don't know which direction it will go, or where the terrifying explosion will happen next.

THOSE were the scariest moments of my life for me, sitting huddled against the wall in our corridor, and every single time a rocket was being fired, there was the excruciating anticipation of wondering IF it was going to hit our apartment building and whether we were going the next ones to die. So, it was really the hissing, zinging, and flying sounds of something being fired and flying through the air that scared me the most.

One of the methods I used to survive my lingering fears from the tumultuous nighttimes was to go into my own imaginary world during the day. I would play with my Barbies and Ken dolls with the horse stable setup and Barbie horses and they would take long trail rides into a forest where it was serene and peaceful. Dreaming about this helped calm me down and pass the time. It was an escape.

In 1976, we left Beirut as war refugees, never to return. I don't know about you, but my family was always one that liked to Sweep Things under the Rug. This meant that we never openly discussed unpleasant things. On the one hand, sweeping things under the rug can be a useful technique without having to think about bad things. On the other hand, I never had the chance to confront my fears of living in Beirut. I've avoided war movies to this day, walked out of the movie Platoon within 5 minutes of it starting, have been afraid of the dark, and have avoided the sound of fireworks for the over 4 decades since we left.

But one thing was clear. Aside from those things, I felt completely fearless and almost invincible. I started to horseback ride in Germany and the most magical thing happened. I found myself in that exact same forest I had daydreamed about. This was a powerful moment and realization that has stuck with me throughout my life. Whenever I wanted something, I would dream big and visualize it happening. I would see myself winning and accepting awards and hearing the applause in the room. This tool of visualization helped me achieve 2 Emmy Awards, 4 Telly Awards, 9 Furniture Design Awards, and 3 Race Car Championships.

The best thing that came from my ex-marriage were two beautiful daughters. Despite trying for many years to keep my failing marriage working, 6 years ago, when I turned 50, I decided to say Enough is Enough. I felt like I had lost who I was and was taking care of everyone else, as we women tend to do. It was on a business trip to Dubai when I was riding an Arabian Horse in the Arabian Desert that I remembered who I was. The girl I had lost along the way. Martina Kwan. I knew at that moment that I would end my marriage, and I also decided to become a race car driver and I named my 911 Firehorse. Anything is possible at any age if you believe in yourself. Making that decision also resulted in finally finding my soulmate and love of my life, Dwain Dement.

It was while I was working on my 3rd Championship in my Porsche 911 in 2019, that I was approached to drive a season in the Saleen S1 race car. I do believe that in life, a lot is being in the right place at the right time. And...I remembered Richard Branson's quote: "If somebody offers you an amazing opportunity but you are not sure you can do it, say yes – then learn how to do it later!" I have used this many times throughout my career in building multiple award-winning businesses.

A few weeks after being first approached by Saleen, we had our first test day at Thermal Racetrack. The S1 is an incredible race car, full of rawness and beautiful strength, agility, horsepower, and a turbocharged engine. I remember getting into the Saleen S1 that day, and quite frankly, feeling…A SURGE OF PARALYZING FEAR. What was it about this machine that frightened me to the core???? What was it about this racecar that prevented me from driving it like my own Porsche 911 racecar? It took me a few months to even identify the fear.

On August 15th, we were doing a test day at Buttonwillow to practice for the 2nd race of the season. I woke up that morning and FINALLY realized what was making me fear the car.

I realized that I had heard the sounds of the car 43 years ago. I realized that I had heard those sounds when I was an 8-10-year-old little girl living in Beirut, Lebanon during the War.

It was the hissing and popping sounds of the racecar that reminded me of the sounds of machine guns, bombs, and rockets hissing and flying through the air, followed by explosions.

I knew I had to get over my fear fast, I knew it was time to no longer sweep things under the rug. It was time for me to pull the rug up and confront the fears I had subconsciously carried around for 4 decades. It was at that moment I pulled off on the highway before the Mountain road known as Grapevine to Buttonwillow and found a video on YouTube with the real sounds of machine-gun fire, rockets, bombs, and explosions. For the first time in over 40 years, I listened to the violent and aggressive sounds that I had heard sitting in that corridor. I listened to these violent sounds for 1 hour at full volume. As I was listening, it made me cry to think of the little 9-year-old girl that I was in Beirut, climbing into my sister's bed every night & remembering the visceral fear that I felt. Having listened to these sounds for an hour at full volume, desensitized me and took away my negative association so that by the time I reached Buttonwillow, I was able to get into the S1 with much less fear than I had before. I got into that racecar and was able to podium twice in 7 races during the season.

Conquering your fears will set you free!

SABINE VOLKMANN

Hypnosis Trainer

https://www.facebook.com/sabine.volkmann.7

https://www.instagram.com/volkmannsabine/

www.hypnose-lueneburg.de

www.hypno3.com

My Name is Sabine Volkmann. Born on April, 30th, 1969 in Hamburg, Germany, and I am the proud mother of two children, Laura & Joshua.

My school years were spent in Hamburg and after school, I studied fashion design. I worked as a pattern designer for well-known sportswear companies, unfortunately, a dying profession in Europe at the time.

After the birth of my daughter, I became a driving instructor and later ran my own driving school. Later, I helped create a driving license learning software. There was an element of hypnosis within the software to help combat test anxiety.

I discovered my real destiny was in the field of Hypnotherapy and energy work. On passing the German state Naturopathy (Psychotherapy practitioner) examination, I opened The Hypnosis Lüneburg practice in 2014. I have been trained by some of the best hypnotists in the world, in accordance with the cause-oriented methods of Dave Elman and Gerald Kein. For several years I ran the OMNI Hypnosis Training Centre in Dublin.

In recent years I developed a concept for driving instructors called the Driving School Mental Coach, which is about giving instructors the tools they need to help students cope with the anxieties of driving and the test exam. As well as treating clients with Hypnotherapy, I also run several courses during the year and lecture at education centers & conferences.

Contact is possible via my homepage www.hypnose-lueneburg.de or E-Mail sabine@hypno3.com

Thrive! How I Found My Calling In The Field of Hypnosis

By Sabine Volkmann

Having read Selena Dorsey's appeal for this book, I thought "Yes!", I want to be involved. Until now, I hadn't considered the evolution of my business success and the obstacles endured. I didn't want the journey to sound negative, even if the outcome was positive – could a balance be found? Life's experiences have made me the person I am today – running a successful hypnotherapy practice and education center.

The truth is, the courage and inspiration you need will come from several sources, helping you to push your way along. Resilience was my key and is something that is within each of us, but it's how we use it, and how we emphasize the key determinants in our overall well-being and quality of life. But more later, first, let me tell you how my story began.

A busy outgoing child, growing up in the center of Hamburg, Germany, I annoyed my parents with my philosophical questions. During our long-distance holidays in Europe, I wondered what was happening behind the many illuminated windows we passed. I asked, could I meet everyone in the world. It's not possible they said – it would be 20 years before the birth of the internet. Nonetheless, I always had an inkling we were all connected somehow. And in my heart, I had an indestructible feeling that there was more to explore between heaven and earth, but my father was an atheist and a practical man, and largely forbade thinking in those terms.

At age 12 my parents separated, but I remained close to both. I believe my father wanted a son as he happily encouraged my interest in motorcycles and driving. After school, I studied at the fashion academy and became a pattern designer.

In my passion as a young entrepreneur, an Italian partner and I opened a small fashion boutique in Hamburg. Unfortunately, it didn't work out and it left me with some debt that took a few years to clear.

After marrying, I started working in my husband's driving school and after training and obtaining the required licenses, became a driving instructor. In Germany, a driving instructor must have licenses to drive in all vehicle classes, even in trucks. The marriage fell apart after only a few years and I moved out with my 4-year-old daughter. My son comes from a second attempt at family, but that relationship was also short-lived. I opted for life as a single mom – it would be 10 years before I tried a serious relationship again.

During the early days of computerizing the driving theory systems of the time, I was involved in a startup software company for several years. This was a very difficult time – managing the kids as a single mom and developing the business. Money was tight, very tight! While the experience gained here would be invaluable later, I often wondered if this was the right place. It felt as though I was only using 30% of my inner potential.

Always interested in homeopathy and various forms of energy healing, I started by booking an online Reiki course. However, during the course, the instructor explained it was "Besprechen", an old healing technique. Having to test it out on my daughter at the time, she explained she could feel the energy from my hand. Wow, I had a gift!

My mother later explained that my great-grandfather had this gift too. Seems it had been passed on, although I never knew it. I could cure warts and shingles using this technique. It was fascinating to have this gift, and it worked! And, indeed, I had my first customers! I went on to study Reiki as well as attend the naturopath school.

A regular Reiki customer introduced me to Hypnosis. I attended a session in Hamburg and was quite impressed by the instructor and the methods. This was to be the turning point - it could be more than a hobby!

I attended the first of many Hypnosis courses and for the next two years would run my tiny practice from home. Finally passing the naturopath exam in the summer of 2015, I immediately opened my first practice outside the home. It was very exciting indeed!

At some point it was all too much for my body, I was diagnosed with Grave's disease. After getting over the initial shock, my resilience factor kicked in, and I discovered a new hypnosis technique with outstanding results. My mentor taught me about the world of "cause-oriented hypnosis" and the "Simpson Protocol". I am eternally grateful to him because we could cure my double-vision using these techniques. We attended several International Hypnosis conferences together and later I trained in Florida to become an instructor.

It was, after all, one of the largest Hypnosis schools in the world and on successful completion of the program, I opened my branch in Dublin, Ireland. However, the Corona pandemic ensured the development of my training system. Now, I deliver courses for anxiety prevention while still maintaining the practice in Germany. In my specially designed seminar, driving instructors learn how to free their students from driving and examination anxieties.

There are many reasons why people come to my practice, but it's usually because they haven't processed something or want to change it. The body constantly repairs itself while the soul processes all impressions during sleep or in a trance.

Hypnosis is a trance state, and the therapy aspect is my work. Thus, I place the client into a trance state and then the psychological treatment follows. Therapy is typically about forgiveness, releasing blockages, creating motivation, erasing negative habits, releasing feelings of guilt, strengthening self-confidence, and processing traumas.

Here are a few case examples:

A 38-year-old man had asked if I could make home visits because his social phobia was so extreme he would faint when he walked out the door. He was about to be admitted to a psychiatric clinic.

During hypnosis, I persuaded him to allow the fear to come to the surface and to describe how he felt it on a scale from one to ten. Eight, he said. I could see his carotid artery throbbing as his body trembled.

I moved his subconscious mind to the first situation where he recognized the feeling. He was 8 years old and surrounded by other children in the schoolyard. They teased and bullied him because both his parents were deaf – "a child of stupid parents". His subconscious mind has been afraid of people since the experience. We then worked on this trauma and found his resilience factor. A month later, I received a message that he was going out with his dog again.

The subconscious mind has miraculous and sometimes peculiar ways to protect us. As a Hypnotherapist, not only a good education counts but also the ability to interpret the abstract patterns of the subconscious.

Another example was a 13-year-old girl who had a phobia of snakes. She would not sleep alone. An upcoming overnight school trip was the immediate problem and she refused to go because of her fear. During the initial client conversation, her mother stated that she had not had any experiences with snakes.

On her hypnotic journey, she landed in her mother's womb, squirming, as childbirth was imminent. She could hardly breathe - she said a snake was wrapped around her!

Discussing the birth with the mother after the initial session, she explained her daughter was born with the umbilical cord wrapped around her. There we had the cause.

The cognizance that snakes had not harmed her, helped her to cope and from then on, she slept alone.

Awareness and processing are the keys, but the therapist/client relationship must be one of trust – the client should be open to permitting access to the subconscious.

If you are unhappy with your career or life situation, then listen to your heart. Write down your dreams. Keep picturing it as it should be, not as you fear it might be. Send your goals to the universe. Imagine yourself traveling to that situation in life that makes you happy. The energy always follows the attention. The important thing is to stay with yourself and not try to imitate others. You can, of course, look up to those who have made it, but, live your style.

If there is the slightest chance I, or any of the other great women in here, can inspire you to follow your dream then it was worth it. My life is now more beautiful than ever, and I'm grateful to all those who have contributed to it.

I am at peace with the people and circumstances that have challenged my path, for I am here now – where I want to be!

ADAINA BIGGS

Well-Respected Life Coach / Best-Selling Author /
Entrepreneur and Personal Advisor

https://www.facebook.com/adaina

https://www.instagram.com/adainabiggs/

http://www.adaina.com/

Adaina is an Empowerment Coach currently thriving in Fairhope, Alabama. She has been speaking from stages, encouraging and educating people since 1994. Adaina's career evolved to Health Coach in 2015 just a couple of years after she was able to manage a chronic autoimmune disease into remission. She transitioned from Health Coach to Empowerment Coach in 2018 when she realized that mindset was pivotal for ALL success.

Adaina's approach to addressing the underlying root cause of limiting beliefs might be something you've never heard before. Her story is almost savage. She has overcome more than most and she has a simple 5-step program for helping others free themselves from their current circumstances and old habits. Her love for the oppressed runs deep. You'll feel it anytime you're in her presence.

5 Boundaries To Change Your Life And Grow Your Business

By Adaina Biggs

Life is ripe with opportunity. Always. Whether you are currently thriving or barely surviving, there's an aligned action to take that can significantly impact your trajectory. Boundaries have been one of my greatest realizations in both my business and my personal world.

I grew up poor in South Louisiana. I suffered significant abuse during my childhood, part of which I attributed to being on the lower levels of the socio-economic scale. I grew up in survival mode and learned patterns that transferred into my adult life. I decided at a young age that I would never be poor again and started working full-time at the age of 14. I started my first two businesses at the age of 19. I've been self-employed for most of my adult life and I attribute my successes in business and personal endeavors to my education, experience, and implementation of healthy boundaries.

This is my personal top 5 list for Boundaries that Build Better Businesses. We will cover the quick and simple version here, but the bottom line is: if you implement these things, you can be happier, healthier, and more profitable.

1) Guard your circle - I once had a client with a one-hour commute which meant she spent two hours a day in her car. I asked her what she did with that time. She told me she was always on the phone with "insert relative's name" listening to her complain about her life, her aches and pains, and her lack of ambition. She felt obligated to let this person vent to her for TWO WHOLE HOURS EVERY DAY.

While this is an extreme example, every 30 minutes adds up. You know who I'm talking about.

Who you are and what you achieve are often directly correlated to your "circle of five" (the people you spend the most time with). It's the reason we tell our children not to "hang out with the wrong crowd". If you spend your time with wealthy people, you will become wealthy. If you spend your time with people who watch too much tv, you'll watch too much tv. If you spend your time with people who live joyfully, you are much more likely to be joyful. It's a known fact that we, as women, frequently overlook this because we are sympathetic by nature and want to care for other people (or worse, concern ourselves with being LIKED by other people).

Do you want to be successful and live the life of your dreams? Guard yourself and your time from negative people and negative influences. It's ok to care about and love people who aren't aligned with you. Just don't give them too much of your time. That's a lot of your life you're trading for someone who would rather sit in the crab bucket and complain.

THE BEST thing you can do to help others is to succeed yourself. When others see you transform, they will either follow suit or quietly exit your life to find more people they are aligned with. If it's their season to sit in the mess and complain, let them do it. Just don't allow it on your watch.

Action step: Answer in writing, "Besides me, who's in my circle of five?" Who do you talk to the most? Who do you spend the most time with? Is there anything there that needs to change?

2) **Take regular breaks** - we all know we are more productive when we take breaks. Set aside time (schedule it if you must) to take breaks during your working hours. Go for a walk, have a cup of hot tea, go sit in a space where you can be anonymous, and have your thoughts to yourself.

You know the feeling you get when you're headed out on a road trip and suddenly your life comes into focus and you think things like "I should really be flossing daily" or "I should exercise more" etc. They are things that matter to you in your overall life, but they sometimes escape you in your day-to-day rut. The same applies to smaller breaks during the day. They provide you with a clearer picture of what's most important so you don't get distracted by the minutia.

Action step: Schedule at least one break (not your lunch) for tomorrow's workday.

3) **Practice Visualization** - Yes, for real. I want you to daydream at work (and at home).

Visualization is a tool used by most professionals (including business owners, CEOs, and professional athletes) to see their highest potential and aim for it. In order to do this effectively, you'll need a boundary around this time. It's much less effective with distractions. Schedule a time and put a boundary around it. Make it a priority. Your best life comes from your best realizations. This is why people often have AHA moments in the shower... because they are alone and not looking at their phones or laptops. PRO TIP: keep some bathtub crayons or a dry erase marker in the shower so you can capture these ideas when they flow :)

Action step: Plan to spend ten minutes on visualization immediately upon waking up. If that fails (I know, kids, dogs, etc), schedule it during your workday.

4) Plan Ahead - No one ever gets to a place they don't plan to go. Why would anyone expect otherwise? Let's see.... I need some eggs and onions so why don't I just get in my car and see where it takes me? But, a lot of people spend more time planning their next vacation than they do planning their life or career. What if they put that much effort into their life or business plan? Or even their one-year plan?

Action step: Sit with yourself for 10-20 minutes and decide what you want to accomplish. Set the intention and plan from there. How much time would you spend planning a vacation? Give your business the same or more priority. Again, you need a boundary here. No distractions.

5) Guard your health - this one cannot be overstated. You must put the oxygen mask on yourself first. Self-care is essential for the success of your business. A cluttered mind is like a hamster on a wheel: ninety to nothing and not making a lot of progress. THIS could be a whole book all by itself.

The short version: you know what you need to do to take care of yourself. If you need ME-time or a massage or a wellness visit or therapy or a girl's night. DO IT. We could totally get in the weeds here and talk about things like how important massage is for lymphatic health... but again, you know what YOU need. Stop making excuses for why you can't take care of yourself.

Action step: Make the call. Send the text. Schedule the dang thing.

This might seem over-simplified, but let's do a quick review. If you actually did all these things, how would your business change? How would your life change? It may seem like a lot, but let's break it down into simple "how long does all this really take because it sounds like a lot" talk.

- Number 1 takes one minute. All you have to do is decline a call and send a text saying you're dealing with something. If you have to explain it later, call it a mental health moment. People will usually leave that alone and let you have it.

- Number 2 - if you take two 15-minute breaks during your day that's 30 minutes per day to recharge your brain and allow you to be more effective and more productive.

- Number 3 - Visualization - ten minutes per day

- Number 4 - Planning - Ten minutes a week so that's about two minutes per day.

- Number 5 - Self-Care - I would allow for one hour per day to accommodate appointments or get your walk in or soak in the tub or whatever it is you need on that day.

One through Four are literally less than one hour per day and LOOK AT ALL THE BENEFITS you can get from that. All that's required is for

YOU to value it and to set boundaries around it. If you still think you can't do all that, the core issue is your belief system. You must show up for yourself. You must love yourself. You must value yourself and understand that you are worthy of saying NO or locking your door. If you can only do ONE thing, start with Number 3.

I have tons of tips and tricks for all these steps if you're struggling with them, but a quick search online can return tons of ideas to spark your own creativity.

Get in the game. The real game. Play joyfully and play to win.

I hope to see you in my future! XOXOXO

VENISE MAYBANK, EA, MTAX

Founder and CEO of Elite V Biz and Finance / Tax
Strategist / Crypto and Real Estate Investor

https://elitevbiz.com/

Venise N. Maybank is the Founder and CEO of Elite V Biz and Finance and is known for her expertise in navigating through the maze of tax laws and providing tax solutions for numerous business owners. She mentors and provides guidance to clients by helping them to build and protect wealth through wealth management and tax strategies. She provides tax remedies that are overlooked in today's world. Venise has over 25 years of experience in tax preparation, planning, and integral in numerous levels of financial accounting. Venise continues to steer companies into setting up the right legal structure for their business for greater wealth and success.

Venise serves as an Enrolled Agent for the Internal Revenue Services and is federally authorized to serve as a tax practitioner empowered by the U.S. Department of the Treasury. Her expertise allows her to represent tax clients on several tax issues including audits, collections, and appeals.

Venise always keeps abreast of the changing times in finance and investment strategies so she fulfills her next passion, real estate, by partnering with some of the greatest investors in the multiunit markets and continues to build a legacy for her family.

Her wealth of knowledge doesn't stop there. As a crypto trader, she is passionate about the new blockchain opportunities, not providing financial advice, but she is passionate about helping others by offering courses in learning more about cryptocurrency and taking their knowledge further into this new era of finance.

Venise lives in sunnyside FL with her family. She loves to travel, cook exquisite meals, and enjoys singing worship music.

Time Value Of Investment Strategies - A Quantum Leap Into A Bright Future

By Venise Maybank

I remember growing up watching a futuristic cartoon called The Jetsons, a family of four whose housing was in the sky, and they drove aero cars that looked like flying saucers and had a robotic maid and a talking dog. This was the perfect view of a utopian family. The parents George and Elena worked a three-day workweek leaving them the convenience of enjoying time with their two children Judy and Elroy. Although the first episode was aired back in 1962, it took us into a time of 2062 where one can only imagine what the future holds for technology and how fast-paced our society is evolving with new trends, new rising developments, and especially the new web 3.0 buzz that is taking over the internet world. This brings me to why I decided to look deeper into why the topic of this book is **The Time Value of Investment Strategies** is now probably the best time based on the era we are now living in.

I am so grateful for the opportunity to be a part of the collaboration and co-writing with these dynamic ladies. I want to personally thank Selena Dorsey for executing her vision and allowing me to be a part of it. I truly hope the information written will be eye-opening and brings us a step further in planning for what's to come.

I purposely reflected on the time value of things and where the world is today. Bartering was an old method of exchange where people exchanged goods for services long before money was introduced. The bartering system eventually faded, then came the gold standard and eventually the fiat, also known as cash which became our main medium of exchange. Fast forward we are now living in a society where some places no longer accept cash. Seems we are heading into a cashless society as some places only accept credit cards. Satoshi Nakamoto, the developer of Bitcoin introduced us to cryptocurrency back in 2008, and this too is now another form of exchange that is gradually scaling in today's society. The age of decentralized cryptocurrency is upon us and who knows, talks of traveling to Mars seem to be a key element where the dollar will be of no use in space. Instead of bartering goods and services, using fiat or even credit cards for that matter, a new way to send money over the internet only makes sense for the introduction of bitcoin and the thousands of other coins on many exchange platforms. Not only are we also talking about trips, but I feel we are also living in a time where we could be close to living in a reality world like the Jetsons.

We see here that the value of money has changed over centuries and it somewhat forces us to think of where we will be financially with all these changes. The dollar may eventually be utilized less or may fade like the bartering system. The story of the Jetson sparked an interest in me having a three-day workweek and spending quality time with my family, going on vacations, or even being my own boss. As a tax strategist who is passionate about managing finances and exploring unique ways to make your dollar work more for you, I demonstrate ways one can eliminate paying too many taxes. While I am not writing this book to give financial advice, it makes sense for us to start adapting to the way society is changing and exploring an ideal plan that will allow us to be a part of this fast-paced technology and ever-changing society.

As a believer, God who is the author and finisher of my faith, says in one of my favorite books in the bible Proverbs 29:18 "Where there is no vision, the people perish" I know this sounds like doom and gloom but it makes sense. How else would the Jetson work three days a week and have quality time to spend with their family on the nonworking days without living out something they probably planned or anticipated what their everyday living should be. A plan is a vision, and if you don't have a vision then you cannot execute a plan. I love the word plan, and another favorite scripture for me is found in Jeremiah 29:11 which states "For I know the plans I have for you declares, the Lord, plans to prosper you and not to harm you, but to give you hope and a future. Even though no one can necessarily know what tomorrow brings forth, I believe as we move through time, our purpose is to write the vision, make it plain, set our goals, and plan for the future.

The time value of investment strategies can help us reach that financial goal for ourselves and our families. Keeping funds or cash in the bank is probably not a futuristic way to make our money grow for us. There are so many avenues one can invest in today. I saw a Jetson moment where I too want to ensure I have that time to spend with my family and work a few days a week. So, I started to follow the trend of where the future is taking us and diversified my investment portfolio. Real Estate is one of the most promising forms of investment that one could venture into today. Like any investment, there are risks, and real estate sometimes fluctuates but recently it has shown to be a high-demand asset investment that one would want to add to their investment portfolio. The low inventory of available properties and investors rushing to buy properties at whatever cost shows us that there will always be a future in real estate and a sure way for your investment to grow over time.

Cryptocurrency is now being introduced also as a medium of exchange in banks and other retail platforms, and it only lets you know that the future is rapidly changing and not having a strategy or partaking in some of these investments can really set you back in time. Just like the time value of money, the time value of investments into stocks, solo 401K's, bonds, crypto, real estate, or even an investment into advancing yourself and having your own business. Knowledge is a gift, not only is it a gift, but it is everything, and I believe we are all on this planet to be creators. Your gift opens the way and brings you before great men. Your gift can be your hobby, and your hobby can be the channel for you to start. Solving a problem, creating a business from it, and using your profit to invest in your future. It's your vision that you are putting into action.

So, was the Jetson giving us a hint of where we are now? As the scriptures read "plans to prosper; to give you hope and a future" God made us creators to prosper and we cannot accomplish a goal without a vision and without a strategy. I can only imagine what the future holds so I want to be sure my thoughts are in line with what God has in store for me based on what he states in his word.

So, if you have not written a plan, maybe search and watch an episode of the Jetson and imagine if you are living in their time, are you holding their medium of exchange, did you let your money sit in the bank and earning you little to no interest or you find out the cash that you have been saving for years no longer is accepted. Your investment strategy should be mapped out with key investments that can take you there. The Internal Revenue Service now has a line specifically asking if you have invested in cryptocurrency on the first page of form 1040. While they tend to update and change their forms most years, a question about cryptocurrency only shows that the government is also adapting to this change and maybe hinting to us that crypto is here to stay. What medium of exchange are you using? Did you set up your company and started solving a problem?

Time waits on no one so having a strategy that is conducive in today's time, having a plan, and creating then executing a financial path for you and your family is the greatest gift one could give to their offspring. Your business can be a legacy that you can pass on to them. It sets the precedents for them to invest in themselves and helps them to take charge of their own future. It gives them the right to walk in your vision and your plan and then eventually start a vision on their own.

The right timeline is now and your investment strategy is the solid pathway for a brighter future.

TATIANA VILAREA

Trauma-Integrative Hypnotherapist / Intuitive and Coach

https://www.facebook.com/tatianavilareahypnotherapy

https://www.instagram.com/tatianavilareahypnotherapy

Tatiana Vilarea is a trauma-integrative hypnotherapist, intuitive, and coach who helps purpose-driven female entrepreneurs and leaders overcome emotional wounds and trauma that show up as business blocks, so they can fully step into their visibility, confidence, impact, and financial success. As a result of her personal journey and over 10 years of experience working with emotional healing, she developed a highly effective modality that releases negative emotions and traumatic memories stored in the body's neurological patterning and cellular memory, that she combines with subconscious work.

Tatiana is passionate about guiding her clients to the emotional and mental freedom they need to reach their personal and professional goals while building success on the foundation of deep self-trust, emotional well-being, and rock-solid confidence.

When she is not helping entrepreneurs get to their dreams, she is busy pursuing her passion for spirituality and psychology, while traveling the world for 4.5 years.

Wherever We Go, We Take Ourselves With Us

By Tatiana Vilarea

Have you ever felt that you are hitting a wall trying to reach a goal in your business?

This was my daily experience for the first three years after starting my business. Even though I had experienced a huge transformation using hypnotherapy and was driven to share it with the world, underneath it all, I was absolutely terrified of being seen and known for my work.

You see, I moved to America alone, at age 19, trying to escape the family nightmare I was living in. I thought I could just run away and start life from scratch. Instead, my past continued to silently affect every decision, relationship, and the job I had, year after year. Rock bottom after rock bottom.

Yet none of it compared to the roller coaster ride that entrepreneurship would become for me. Back then, I had no idea that starting and growing a business would trigger and surface every fear and block I have ever had. Magnified tenfold.

My biggest ones were fear of the camera and public speaking. Every time I tried going on camera or speaking in front of people, I would feel paralyzing fear and could barely breathe or move my body, no matter how much I practiced. And because I was anticipating it, I lived in a constant state of stress.

In addition to it, since this fear affects much more than just showing up on camera and public speaking when it comes to running a business, I was resisting or avoiding all marketing and self-promotion. Which also included selling—I hated sales calls!

Needless to say, I wasn't able to show up consistently, reach people or be the leader I truly wanted to be.

In the beginning, I did all the "right things". I invested in multiple coaches, learned business and marketing strategies, and tried to push through my fear to grow my business. I also went from one practitioner to another trying to change my subconscious beliefs about being seen. I persisted, hoped, and dreamed. But felt stuck and kept hitting the same wall over and over again.

While most importantly, there I was, a hypnotherapist who could not overcome my own fear. No matter what results I was able to create for my clients at the time, this inner struggle was affecting my confidence and belief in myself.

Three nerve-racking years into my business, I was living in a basement apartment that had one tiny window, going insane from the non-stop noise made by my upstairs neighbors. I was $15,000 in debt. This meant that it was time to either give up on my dreams and start looking for a job or change whatever I was doing since it was obvious that I was missing a big piece of this puzzle.

Until one moment, after yet another session with a new hypnosis practitioner I hired, I had a realization that forever changed the trajectory of my business and life. I finally saw that I was trying to fix the wrong problem: I was working on changing my beliefs and reprogramming my subconscious mind, but the paralyzing fear lived in my body! It was my body that went into a state of panic every time I was going to be visible.

My body remembered the pain I went through as a child and other trauma that I tried to run away from by moving to the United States. So, because my body perceived being seen as a similar "threat", it was trying to preserve itself and kept bringing up all sorts of sabotage and resistance to ensure its safety.

For the next several years, I embarked on a journey to study trauma and its effect on the body and the nervous system. The more I learned, the more convinced I became that there was a direct connection between traumatic experiences, nervous system dysregulation, and, as a consequence, many fears, blocks, and limitations we struggle with in our personal and professional lives. I also discovered that leading trauma experts are now teaching this body-based approach to trauma work.

I knew I had to move away from trying to fix my mind or the "symptoms" I experienced in my business and begin addressing the real causes beneath the surface: the trauma and the state of unsafety that were hard-wired into my nervous system and its neurological patterning.

It was no longer a surprise to me that I could never fully release the reactions my body was having with the mind alone since we cannot override the autonomic nervous system and body's intelligence with thinking, reasoning, or willpower. This biological process is beyond our intellectual control.

My entrepreneurship journey became a quest and the deepest process of personal growth and transformation I have ever experienced.

And since none of the techniques and modalities I had tried worked for me, I decided to do what I now know I do best: improvise and innovate.

Using my background in psychology, education in trauma work, and personal discoveries, I went on to develop a unique way of working with the nervous system and body "memory".

It was a process that could be understood by the body because it went beyond words, reasoning, and logic.

I started to believe that there was a different, kinder, and more sustainable way of doing business for my physical and mental health.

Moreover, as I was going through this transformation in my own body, life and business, I began to recognize the same patterns in other women I was working with, in how they avoided being seen, how their emotional wounds and hidden trauma affected their confidence, self-trust, personal and professional relationships. It impacted their ability to make more money, and share their message on a larger scale, especially for those who have gone through childhood, family or sexual trauma, and other adverse life experiences.

As women, we also experience cultural, social, and transgenerational factors that have historically contributed to a state of fear and an overall sense of lack of safety and security. Without a physical, felt experience of safety, our nervous systems, minds, and bodies cannot function optimally and we remain in a state of hyper-vigilance and, ultimately, survival. This is why the most common "symptoms" experienced by female entrepreneurs are stress, burnout, anxiety, inability to relax, and overwhelming worry about the future and finances.

All these experiences create a lot of business challenges, unconsciously sabotage our success and make strategy implementation more difficult. We are often told to just push through our fears and "do it anyway". We hear that it will get better with practice and that changing our mindset around visibility, selling, marketing, and money is the main solution for overcoming these blocks. And of course, these steps are important. But, just as if we were building a house—no matter how great our walls and other materials are—without a solid foundation, it will not stand strong.

Without this foundational work, we continue to spend energy on fighting our inner battles, try to compensate with strategies and actions, and deplete ourselves as a result. Entrepreneurship becomes exhausting and the price we pay for success is too high.

However, when I began addressing my trauma and those deeper survival patterns, everything began to change rapidly. What was even more fascinating, is that once the body memory was released and my nervous system stabilized, my beliefs and actions began to change organically. I was no longer reacting to the old triggers and began feeling real freedom to take consistent actions and implement all the strategies I had studied.

Moreover, I finally began to enjoy running my business. I now show up fully and look forward to every opportunity to get in front of people, so I can make an impact in other women's lives and help them get to the emotional and mental freedom they need in order to achieve their goals. With my support, they can fully step into their visibility, confidence, and expertise to share their work on a larger scale, while creating financial independence and freedom for themselves and their families.

I truly believe that women are meant to lead this world to a new future.

And only by going through a process of deep inner healing and transformation, can we face our fears, overcome any challenges, and awaken to our embodied wisdom, self-awareness, and self-mastery that are needed for this next-level leadership.

Grounded in our power. Solid in our Purpose.

Fearless.

BESSIE ESTONACTOC, MA, ACHT

Spiritual Coach / Hypnotherapist / Healer

https://www.facebook.com/bessieestonactocspiritualcoach

www.BessieEstonactoc.com

As a former relationship therapist for 20 years, Bessie has helped hundreds of spiritual mid-life businesswomen and women entrepreneurs who have felt overwhelmed because they were juggling their business/work while caring for their relationship with their loved ones, especially their ailing parents. Bessie has taught women holistic, actionable steps and strategies to find peace, and heal their relationships and themselves.

Being an entrepreneur, Bessie learned firsthand how resilience, faith, and surrender deepened her relationship with her ailing mother while becoming even closer to her husband of 41 years.

Holy Crap!!! Can I Really Do This?
A Business Woman's Journey To Finding Peace In Chaos

By Bessie Estonactoc

I just started to doze off for the night into slumberland and then I heard the cowbell ring. I woke up startled, realizing how late it was. Not again, I thought to myself. I wanted to get up early to prepare for work but maybe work wasn't going to happen today. At this point, I was a caregiver for my mother, so my time wasn't my own.

With my eyes barely open I walked over to my mother's bedroom to find out what was happening with her.

The cowbell was my mother's call for assistance. It meant she wasn't feeling well, and the sound of it sent me into fear and panic, not knowing what she needed, how I could help, or what it might entail.

You see, back in 2005 my husband and I were empty nesters AND in the "sandwich" generation. Our son was on his own with the military, our daughter was full-time in college and we were supporting her financially. Since it was just hubby and me in our home, I enjoyed going on dates or last-minute trips to the mainland with him. I FELT CAREFREE!

But my mother was at a point with her health where she needed a safe place to live and be monitored more closely and I wanted her to live with me and my husband so I could help her.

After having a conversation with my husband about this, he was totally willing to have her with us at our home on Oahu. My family values were so strong that of course, I felt it only right to have mom live with us. But deep down, I did say to myself "Holy Crap! Can I really do this?" But with blind faith mom moved in.

The first few years were wonderful with her! She was still ambulatory and was ALL over Oahu by bus. She loved watching her Korean shows on television and she even joined the Korean Club! She made me smile when I saw her enjoy the new things she did independently while living in Hawaii. We even enjoyed many holidays together! My heart was happy that she was happy.

Then after five years or so of living with us, mom's health was beginning to go downhill. Because she no longer could go to the appointments on her own, I took mom to numerous doctor appointments which took me away from my business.

Being a psychotherapist I was working with clients getting paid for each session. My business relied on me seeing the clients in person. (This was before the zoom days!)

As a result of taking mom around, I had a decline in my income AND then my husband was laid off from not one but TWO jobs! We had to tighten our budget which meant I no longer felt carefree.

Here I was, feeling so stressed and overwhelmed! I was constantly worried, asking myself "Will we run out of money? Will we have enough money in our reserves to last us? Will we be able to continue to help our daughter in grad school?"

There were many sleepless nights when I asked myself these questions. I felt so confused, worried, and numb about the future and my business. How in the world could I get through this????

My mom was relying on me and my husband to help her so she was the priority. I slowly began to feel very burned out between worrying about money and worrying about my mom.

Mom's health was declining even further. Now it was hospital stays, MORE doctor appointments, and 911 calls when she needed to go to the emergency room.

To make it easier and faster to hear when my mother needed help, I got her a cowbell for her to ring which was a way of communicating her needs. My client load continued to dramatically decrease and my husband still didn't have a job. We worried but still kept our commitment to take the best care of mom that we could.

One day I was in a quiet, meditative space. I realized that how I was feeling really wasn't serving me. My energy was depleted. I was acting like a worrywart and I didn't like feeling this way! I realized that I took my mother in to live with us not just because of feeling like it was expected of me, but because I CHOSE to do that. That understanding opened something up.

The affirmation "I let go and I let God' came through in my mind. I have always known that there's an energy bigger than me, call it God, Source, the Divine, and in my moment of stillness, I was reminded of this.

I had been holding on to the fear of the unknown and losing our money, our home, not being able to take care of our daughter in grad school, losing my business, as well as hubby not finding a job and it was killing me. I finally realized that this fear was holding me back from being lovingly present for my mom in the years she had left with us. And I reminded myself that I CHOSE this.

Once I had these realizations, I LET GO of any fears that I had and focused on my mother. My heart was open knowing that I've always been provided for and always will be. I chose to be focused on being grateful that we had reserves to fall back on. I chose to focus on being grateful that I was able to be lovingly present to my mom to have her years more comfortable as possible. I didn't want to have ANY regrets in the years left that mom was with us!

Wow!!! What a carefree feeling this was once I surrendered to this wisdom. By the way, this one thing, gratitude and the remembering that you are always taken care of can carry you through hard situations!

So the sixth and seventh year with mom was so much easier for me emotionally and energetically even though mom's health was not good. Any time that cowbell rang I was ready, willing, and able to wake up in the middle of the night to find out what she needed. I was prepared to call 911, go with her to the emergency room, and not go to work. It was totally fine that my caseload decreased because I knew that the Universe has and always would take care of me and my family. My mom's care was a priority over everything.

Mom and I had heartfelt conversations in these later years about death and dying, making preparations and wishes on how she wanted her service. This was a hard conversation to have with my mother, but I knew I had to broach this subject with her in a loving way. Mom did tell me she was afraid to die but I told her that I promised I would be with her until her last breath.

One day I decided to broach the topic of what kind of service she wanted when she passed away. I mentioned to her that if she could tell me what kind of service she wanted, it would help me, but most importantly have her feel a part of this process. I could tell she felt good about being asked and I felt relieved that she was open to the discussion.

In fact, she was the one that called a local mortuary to have someone come to our home to discuss this topic! I was totally surprised mom took the initiative. Mom made all the decisions and wishes down to the music and the type of urn. And the urn she chose was beautiful.

The energy in our home was more peaceful, hopeful, and filled with love and compassion instead of worry and angst about the future. My energy was more centered and balanced. I was able to be beautifully present with my mom, moment by moment. I truly felt freedom within me and totally supported by the Universe.

Towards the last half of mom's seventh year, she was in a care home, no longer able to sit or stand on her own. She had a walker that would help her but she needed to be watched 24/7 by professional caregivers. Mom's final care home provider was a wonderful woman who was also a hospice nurse. How lucky mom was.

On August 22, 2012, mom called me and said, "Bess, it's time." So I immediately dropped what I was doing and was by mom's side all night massaging her heart, her arms, hands, feet, and legs, giving her Reiki. My husband was by my side supporting me. On August 23, 2012, mom took her last breath on earth and her first breath in the heavens. I fulfilled my promise and I was with her.

Thank you mom for being my teacher to learn how to trust, forgive, surrender and be in compassionate, unconditional love for you.

My hope is that you too realize that gratitude and faith can get you through anything.

To find out about your energy, take my "Relationship Energy Quiz" here:

https://lnk.quizzes.cx/energy-alignment-quiz-with-bessie-estonactoc

VIVIAN DE CAMPBELL

Gifted Teacher / Empowerment Coach

https://bit.ly/3uwSLUs

https://bit.ly/3uoGYYm

Vivian De Campbell is a gifted teacher and life coach. She has been involved in the cutting edge of the personal growth field for 25+ years.

Although she has worked in a variety of settings, her approach always emphasizes the positive.

She has an uncanny ability to help her clients become aware of their own gifts and to use them in making a contribution to others while manifesting their best life.

She has had consecutive successful careers in financial services, winning numerous awards within a fortune 100 company, for years. She has also had a rewarding career as a hospice nurse, using her compassionate communication and nursing skills to bring comfort to both patients and their loved ones

Vivian has been personally trained by some of the leaders in the transformational industry. She was initiated into Reiki by Grand Master Hawaya Takata when she brought Usui Reiki to the USA. Vivian is herself a Reiki Master/Teacher as well as EFT/TFT Master Practioner and Certified Advanced Ho'oponopono Practitioner. She has appeared on Oprah and has led relationship seminars that produced long-lasting unions. She facilitates virtual and in-person seminars on a variety of transformative topics. Contact for personal private sessions or subscribe to her newsletter.

Wow! Imagine That! "The Power To Manifest Everything You Desire. Quicker Than You Ever Thought Possible!"

By Vivian De Campbell

Here's a brief true story.

I visited my girlfriends in Florida for my birthday in November 2016. I was flying home on a 6 AM flight. I was hoping to catch some zzz's on the 2-hour flight home to Chicago. It wasn't a full flight. There was a seat between me and the man seated on the aisle seat. We were about to depart when a lady rushed in.

She asked if the vacant seat was taken. The moment she sat down, she began to talk with the man in the aisle seat for an hour. She then turns her attention to me. She asked if I lived in Orlando or Chicago.

I told her about my brief trip. She was going home to visit her mom. She had a family and had lived in a suburb of Orlando for 14 years. She said her family always tried to get them to move back. She said she loved it there. I said that I always thought of being a snowbird. That's all I had to say. She immediately had me take my phone out and begin writing down the names of places she said that I should look. Long story short...Two days later I found a lovely 2 bedroom, 2 bathroom house in Winter Springs Florida in a charming 55+ community online. I worked with a lovely realtor and on January 17, 2017, I purchased my second home and became a snowbird. Well, Imagine that!

Two years prior I had talked with my life coach about how much I could not abide the harsh winters in Chicago. I had made a vision board for change. Mickey and Minnie Mouse were there for love. Apparently drawing the Orlando vibe as well.

We generally look outside of ourselves for sustenance and meaning. To look beyond the self for power, love, prosperity, happiness, and fulfillment; the fashionable clothes, fabulous cars, gorgeous house, or homes. These achievements are outside ourselves. But is this entirely true?

There is a power that dwells within all individuals. Physically it causes you to breathe and your heart to beat. The electromagnetic energy causes your heart to beat as well as all other bodily functions.

The inner aspect of this energy is passive but can be awakened via your subconscious mind.

This divine energy is the same energy that keeps our physical being alive and functioning. This Universal Intelligence is the Source of Everything. Let me explain.

When you acknowledge your sacred self called Universal Intelligence you are on a journey to enlightenment.

Learning how being one with the Source of All enables you to manifest your desires. I suggest that you Dream Big!

In my interpretation, spirituality is not dogma or rules. I call the journey to experience your sacred self one of transformation. Transformative Living is blissful. Looking inward and discovering why you are here instead of only looking outwardly for external sustenance, satisfaction, and answers.

Upon conception, we chose to make this journey here, we chose these parents and this life. There will be another moment when we proceed from "now here" to "nowhere" and it is called death.

The inner self is simply the term that covers the spirit and the mind and the outer self is a term that describes the physical body and social relatedness.

There are countless ways to communicate with Universal Intelligence for illustration purposes I'll share two in this discussion.

In the Torah, which is the first five books of the Old Testament, it is written "And God said unto Moses, I Am That I Am: and he said, Thus shalt thou say unto the children of Israel, I Am hath sent me unto you" (Exodus 3:7–8, 13–14).

The vibratory sound of these words "I am that I am" doesn't just resonate with Universal Intelligence, it is The Source. This has been called the most powerful manifestation tool in the history of the world.

When stating "I am" anything/word that follows will be manifested, positively or negatively. You must stand watch over your words.

As I desire to transcend this mortal realm I use my "I am" statements. I am love. I am peace. I am understanding. I am wealthy. I am source. I am truth. I am fearless. I am creative. I am vital.

Prepare for Success:

1. List your major desires

2. Optimize your health and well-being

3. Measure your progress

4. Visualize your goals daily

5. Activate your subconscious mind with images of your desires. Vision Boards. Pictures on a wall

6. Persevere until you reach your goals. Don't stop

7. Guard your mouth.

8. Stay positive.

9. Be grateful.

10. Be of service to others.

How to:

Get comfortable in a seated position. (If you recline you may fall asleep) Quiet the body, and make it as comfortable as possible. Close your eyes. Tilt your chin slightly upward. Close your outer eyes and open your inner eye.

Take several deep breaths.

Begin by saying "I am that" while exhaling. On the inhalation say the second "I am". Continuing with this same pattern of repeating the words with the breath Inhalation and exhalation. This time when you say "that" see it in your mind's eye. When you say the second "I am" while inhaling you see and feel "that" already being manifested in your life. Repetition here is fine. Bring Joy to this experience. To anchor this moment, grab your wrist and say "Peace".

Clarification: When you say whatever that is…. see the active picture with you in it as "that" in your mind's eye.

The second manifestation process comes from the Nichiren Shoshu Buddhist tradition.

What is a mantra?

(originally in Hinduism and Buddhism) a word or sound repeated to aid concentration in meditation.

Benefits of chanting (repeatedly saying) Nam Myoho Renge Kyo

It gives strength and the ability to face any problem and difficulties. … The mantra helps to overcome Fear and Phobia. Through this mantra, we dedicate and surrender to the Almighty- the Supreme Power which relaxes the mind and body. It enlightened the Mind.

It is said that Music has the power to heal, to calm the mind, we have all experienced it. But when we combine music with the sound of our chants, we enhance the effect of music 1,000 times. The sound, the vibration of our own voice sends these healing vibrations throughout our body.

Nam Myoho Renge Kyo – Mantra Meaning:

Nam comes from the Sanskrit namas, meaning to devote or dedicate oneself.

Myo can be translated as mystic or wonderful, and ho means law. This law is called mystic because it is difficult to comprehend. It is the Law of Cause and Effect.

Thank Renge means lotus blossom.

Kyo literally means sutra and here indicates the Mystic Law likened to a lotus flower, the fundamental law that permeates life and the universe, the eternal truth.

Devotion to the Mystic Law of the Lotus Sutra or Glory to the Sutra of the Lotus of the Supreme Law. This Mantra suggests for us to surrender and dedicate ourselves to the Name of One Supreme Power – The Mystic Law which itself being blossomed like a Lotus makes us blossom and we feel happy, beautiful, and energetic-full of life-ever young. When we dedicate ourselves to that One Whole of which we are all part, all our sufferings are removed.

It is with great pleasure that I share this Spiritual practice with you dear reader. I am in my 35th year of chanting Nam myoho renge kyo. Many wonderful and mystical experiences and benefits have happened to me in all that time. My favorite quote is "Suffer what there is to suffer. Enjoy what there is to enjoy. Treat both suffering and joy as facts of Life and continue chanting Nam Myoho Renge Kyo to insure happiness in this life and the next."

This quote is from the 13th Century Buddhist monk Nichiren who was the first to chant this Mantra from the Lotus Sutra which was written by Shakyamuni Buddha in the 3rd Century B.C.

The person who shared this practice with me said that I need to show actual proof that it works.

I was told to write down 10 things that I desired. Set aside time to chant each day. Begin with 5-10 minutes morning and evening. After seeing the benefits if you'd like more information about this spiritual practice there is a Buddhist lay organization that began in Japan. The Soka Gakkai which means "Value Creating" There are millions of practitioners all over the planet. SGI-USA is here in the states.

The purpose of all transformative disciplines is for you to be happy. That is what I wish for you as your most empowered self.

SABINE CHARLES

Entrepreneur / Motivational Speaker / Board Advisor
/ Exam-Prep Expert

https://www.linkedin.com/in/sabine-charles/

https://www.youtube.com/channel/UCVGzmbpEuPt3ByKuJ7HjWGw

Sabine Charles is an entrepreneur, motivational speaker, board advisor, and exam-prep expert. Sabine has over 20 years of experience in internal audit, accounting, and risk management. She has proven leadership and results-driven success advising fortune 500 senior executives in Internal Audit Controls, Business Risk, Fraud Investigation, and Operational Auditing. Her "Big 4" background contributes to her level of expertise and successful collaborative approach in building financial infrastructure and refining audit systems that improve productivity, reduce cost, and stimulate growth. She offers a broad range of knowledge with extensive expertise in global operations, information technology audit, investigations, and accounting in financial services and higher education industries. Her previous places of employment include Deloitte, Citibank, and American Express.

Sabine is regarded as an extraordinary communicator, fluent in five (5) languages with the ability to engage at all levels and on a global stage. Considered an industry expert and highly effective at coaching and motivating individuals to perform at their fullest potential, Sabine is a highly sought speaker at conferences, workshops, business meetings, podcasts, and lectures.

She published her first book "Cracking the Code: Techniques for Certification Exam Success" in 2020, which provides clear and concise techniques to help maximize productivity and optimize professionals' time when preparing for certification exams.

Most importantly, she helps them pass!

It's A Bean's Life

By Sabine Charles

I was dethroned! My family came from the country of mountains, where people believe in equality, freedom, and prosperity. The land of my people consists mainly of rugged mountains interspersed with small coastal plains and river valleys. My mom and dad left this beautiful land due to political unrest. I was born in America, Brooklyn, New York, the city of politics, economy, and culture. As I was raised by my parents, their heritage influenced the way I navigate my life.

It was my grandmother who first instilled in me the power of perseverance. She also emphasized other valuable traits such as self-awareness, personal development, and focus on developing others. She knew these attributes would serve me well in all my pursuits. Let me tell you about a time my grandmother greatly impacted me.

On a hot summer's day in the projects in Brooklyn, New York, my grandmother took my brother and me outside to sit in the courtyard to feel the breeze since we did not have central air in our home. It was quite humid. My grandmother sat in her favorite lawn chair and fanned herself while we played a few rounds of bingo. She watched me eyeing some girls my age playing hopscotch and encouraged me to go talk to them. I was so excited; I grabbed my jump rope, which I took with me everywhere, and ran down to the group of girls.

Moments later, I came running back to my brother and grandmother crying. My grandmother did not understand why I was crying because she spoke Haitian Creole, and I spoke English. My brother translated for her that the girls down the street stole my jump rope from me. Her eyes pierced through mine, and she gave me orders to go back and retrieve the rope, or she would give me something to cry about!

With the fear of my grandmother in my heart, I went toward the girls with determination. Confronting the young girls seemed less frightening than my grandmother. Wiping my tears, I confidently told the girls, "I need you to give me my rope back – right now." They did so without hesitation, and I could see the surprise in their eyes when I demanded the rope back. Their initial perception of me was as timid and that I would never stand up for myself. I went back to my grandmother and held my jump rope up triumphantly in front of her. She smiled at me, nodding her head.

That was my first life lesson; Do not let people take things that belong to you and always stand up for yourself.

Growing up multicultural was difficult, especially during my teenage years. I often felt I didn't fit in either culture; exiled, as it were. I did what was required of me. I went to school, stayed out of trouble, graduated college, and eventually landed a great job. But confusion and uncertainty plagued me as a teen and loneliness when my struggle was not understood by those around me. As an adult, I traveled around the world hoping to figure out who I was. I learned and spoke five different languages to understand the various cultures I visited. From all of this, I realized that the journey is not out there, but must begin from within.

Perseverance is the key to success! Exploration and understanding of self are important for developing a growth mindset. Achievement and fulfillment are the rewards that follow you through life. And I think about certifications in the same light. They are the incentives that follow exploring knowledge and gaining skills in business.

10 years ago, when I landed my dream job of running an internal audit department, my employer had one stipulation; that I pursue my Certified Internal Auditor (CIA) designation. My employment contract stipulated that I had a year to complete the exam or be let go. The idea that I would lose my job if I failed this exam caused me a lot of stress. In fact, so much so that I failed the exam many times!

My certification journey involved attending many review classes, self-help seminars, many sleepless nights studying, and finally, crying when I passed the CIA exam. Throughout this process, I developed self-awareness and a method that I realized that I had to share with others. I created learning and stress management techniques that helped me not only pass the CIA exam, but to achieve 12 additional certifications in the areas of information technology, auditing, and risk management. The power of the subconscious mind helped me gain confidence and vision while my newly developed learning techniques equipped me to pass my certification exams.

One day I received a phone call from a potential client who wanted to buy some time with me to tutor her son. She was in Israel and her friend's daughter used my services to become certified and highly recommended my services. But there was one problem. I had no way of receiving electronic payments. I got her email address and told her that I will send her my payment information shortly. That night I created my website and established my payment method. Now fast forward to today... To help others I decided to build a business called TAPA Institute where professionals could review and master the core concepts of accounting, develop a relaxed state of mind, and reinvent their studying and test-taking techniques for certification exams. We are successful because our clients are successful!

My passion for the profession and learning led me to publish my first book which is on Amazon's bestseller list called "Cracking the Code: Techniques for Certification Exam Success". It features clear and concise techniques to uniquely prepare clients for certification exams; and most importantly, to pass!

So, I realized that I was never dethroned, I just never claimed my position on the throne... as the main character in my story.

In conclusion, depending on how you define success, there are steps to help you accomplish your goals. I have learned that you are never too young or old to follow your dreams. I can do anything I put my mind to at any time. Even when I'm going through obstacles and feel like giving in, I encourage myself to be better. This is what I have learned as I go through my journey of life - no matter how tough, everyone's journey is paved differently. No matter what life throws at you, every obstacle is an opportunity to learn, and a blessing to uncover.

DR. BIRGIT ZOTTMANN

Certified hypnotherapist / Hypnosis Instructor /
Certified Strategy Coach / MBSR Teacher (Mindful
Based Stress Reduction) / EMDR practitioner (Eye
Movement Desensitization and Reprocessing) / Yoga
Teacher

www.hypnose-drzottmann.com

Dr. Birgit Zottmann studied psychology, educational science, and humanities in Frankfurt, Germany. She trained in Hypnotherapy with the best teachers in Germany, the UK, and the US.

Dr. Zottmann is also a Mindfulness Teacher (MBSR) (Center for Mindfulness University of Massachusetts) and a Strategic Coach (Tony Robbins)

She has a private practice in Frankfurt, Germany, which has been running for over 20 years. She draws her treatments from a variety of approaches and applies them depending on the client's needs.

She studied pedagogy, sociology, and psychology in Frankfurt am Main.

She is a Hypnosis trainer for the NGH, EMDR Practitioner, and Ego State Therapy Practitioner (Maggie Philipps)

She Lectures in Europe and America

Fake It Till You Make It And Improve Your Self-Confidence

By Dr. Birgit Zottmann

Would you like to become more confident and overcome your fears and challenges? In the following pages, I describe how I use the "as-if strategy" with my coaching clients.

Ellen Langer, a Harvard psychologist, conducted an experiment in 1979 that was reported in a New York Times Magazine cover story.

For one week, Langer placed eight men in their seventies in an environment exactly as it was 20 years ago. "After that week, both the control and experimental groups showed improvements in physical strength, manual dexterity, gait, posture, perception, memory, cognition, taste perception, hearing, and vision," Langer wrote.

The difference in these men was real! Acting as if time hadn't passed for a week had significant health effects.

What impact might this "as if" strategy have on their lives?

You may be thinking, What nonsense, either I'm like this or I'm not like this. Yes, your conscious mind may say that, however, your subconscious mind sees it differently. Your subconscious mind does not distinguish between "real" and "imagined".

Imagine that you are gleefully biting into a ripe, juicy, fragrant, bright yellow lemon in your mouth now.

What happened?

You have more saliva in your mouth. Your body reacts to the idea of a lemon that is not even in your mouth.

When you see a movie that moves you to tears or makes you tense with fear, it's no different.

All you are seeing is a movie, not reality. And yet your subconscious mind thinks it is real, and you cry.

You are pretending. And you can use that: to achieve your goals, realize your plans and enhance your personal growth. Great, isn't it?

Like any tool or coin, this strategy has two sides: It can be useful, harmful, or simply unethical.

When people pretend to be or have something in order to manipulate other people, it is morally questionable. To me, lying is not an acceptable way to communicate with people.

Pretending to have a degree, knowledge, skill, or money, or pretending to love someone is cheating. Such people are phonies and frauds.

Unfortunately, some coaches teach this strategy. They tell you to pretend that you have money, skills, the ideal partner, the dream job, and/or lots of clients, and then you will get what you want - almost automatically. You just have to imagine it as exactly as possible. Just as it happened to you with the lemon. "Believe it and you will get it." And if you don't get it, or don't reach that goal, they will tell you that you didn't believe in it strongly enough.

Only those self-made gurus get rich in this case. Dreams are important, but dreaming alone will not change the world. Successful people learn, review their habits, and adapt them to their goals. They continue to evolve and have a growth mindset that allows them to make mistakes.

Toxic happiness

In my practice, I often meet people who believe that if you don't have positive feelings all the time, you will become depressed, and sick.

These people often were acting as if they were always happy and in a good mood because they think they are pleasing other people by doing so.

If you pretend to have only good feelings, the negative feelings will become stronger and stronger in the long run. This is also confirmed by scientists.

My attitude makes the poem of Robert Frost clear: "The best way out is through". Living against your feelings and emotions and pretending that you are always happy is not a promising strategy if you want to go through life healthy and confident.

When and how is the as-if strategy helpful?

I come from a low-income family and my parents had a lot of problems. I was the oldest child and I was the "strong" girl. Whenever I felt weak, I would pretend to be strong. This was expected of me at first and happened automatically over time. No matter what I felt, I would pretend and "play" the strong one. This was very useful for my educational and professional career. I was able to graduate from university with a doctorate degree, even though I felt very weak and inadequate most of the time. Later in my life, I learned to give up this strategy in order to be more honest with myself and others. I no longer wanted to be just the "strong one".

Being authentic became my goal and that, for me, means being vulnerable and strong.

Today, I face the challenge of growing older without automatically adopting the negative images of aging. Aging in our society is often described exclusively as a loss: We lose our health, our ability to learn, and our attractiveness. I move and behave as if I were twenty years younger. For example, I often hang out with much younger people and physically exert myself. I practice yoga regularly and learn a new language to keep me mentally and physically agile. We now know that we can make positive physical and mental changes at any age.

Overcome exam anxiety

You have studied a lot and you are thinking about the exam with horror. Maybe you are afraid of not being able to write anything or not being able to make a sound. Then the as-if strategy is really helpful.

Pretend that it is natural that you will celebrate passing the exam. Feel how good you will feel during the exam. Imagine that everything is easy and that you are successful. Imagine each step in detail and feel good about it. You may say to yourself as you do this, "It's nice to show what you can do..... I am sitting or standing very upright...I am full of calm energy....". Start your mental exercise where the fear sets in. This only works if you have done your homework and you are prepared. Having the goal in mind is an "as if" strategy. You act as if you have achieved what you wanted.

The self-talk about "Am I good enough?" and "What if I fail?" then takes on a back seat. When you focus on the successful outcome, you will have much more positive energy.

Self-motivation

I often motivate myself with the "as if" strategy. When I'm a little tired and don't feel like doing something, I imagine the feeling I'll have when I finish the task: That super good feeling after I get my workout done, clean the house, or write this article... Next, I pretend that I have already accomplished my task, and with that good feeling, I begin the task.

Self-confidence through self-compassion

It has been scientifically proven that people who have more self-compassion tend to be happier, have higher life satisfaction and motivation, better relationships, and better physical health, as well as less anxiety and depression. Having compassion for yourself doesn't mean wallowing in self-pity or not being able to admit your own faults. It means adopting a kind, loving attitude toward yourself internally and putting it into action. For example, supporting yourself in difficult times instead of judging yourself.

U.S. researcher Kristin Neff, a pioneer in the field of self-compassion, has developed a whole series of exercises that can strengthen self-compassion. She recommends:

- Stop constantly evaluating and judging yourself.

- Learn to accept yourself as you are, with your strengths, weaknesses, and limitations.

- Realize that you are more than the qualities you judge yourself for.

- Try to look at yourself through the eyes of a wise, compassionate friend who also knows your weaknesses and views you with love and kindness.

- Actively comfort yourself when you are in distress. Give yourself a hug, a pat, a word of encouragement, and express compassion to yourself. Your body will respond.

- When you are not feeling well, try to find out what you really need at that moment. Four questions can help you do this: What am I observing? What am I feeling? What do I need at this moment? What request do I have for myself or for someone else?

Start making one day a week a day of self-compassion! For one day, pretend that you have a lot of compassion for yourself. Do these exercises.

And if it doesn't work out the way you want it to, hug yourself (with the hug, your body produces oxytocin a feel-good hormone).

If you do this for a few weeks, you will get more and more used to it, and over time your behavior and feelings will change.

I am a heroine

If you want to feel confident, pretend for once that you are your favorite heroine. Maybe it's a real person, a person you've read about, or a character from a show.

Stand like your heroine for a moment and then walk as she would walk. Pretend you are her. How does it feel?

Children naturally learn by imitating adults. We can learn this way, too.

Don't just walk like your heroine, act like her. How would she overcome obstacles? How would she react to a mistake she made? Pretend.

You don't have to be the perfect woman and the highlight on Instagram to be confident. Be yourself and pretend to be your own heroine. Do it in a fun and joyful way. Over time, you will feel the difference in your mindset.

We feel with the body

Our body is not just a shell. We are our bodies. And the posture of our body is crucial to our feelings. Sometimes, for example, it is very helpful to wear high heels. Not because they look good, no, you immediately have a different posture.

Do an experiment with yourself once. Sit bent over for a while and try to think of something good in your life, and then stretch your back and sit up straight and try to think of the same thing. Feel the difference! Just changing your posture will give you more confidence!

I wish you all the best

Birgit

BETH KOENIG

Advocate / Educator / Presenter

https://www.facebook.com/bethko/

http://sensoryadvice.org

Beth Koenig is an advocate, educator, and lifelong learner.

After growing up with autism spectrum disorder and advocating for students in the public school districts, she turned her attention toward homeschoolers and private education. She has been tutoring children with special needs for over 20 years, specializing in helping those that are deaf, blind, or autistic. In May of 2020, she launched an online preschool that focuses on teaching using sign language and spoken English simultaneously. Not being one to leave out older children, she then started a virtual homeschool enrichment program in September of 2020. Making the most of her experience, she is preparing to launch a virtual private school in September of 2022 to help children who don't benefit from a traditional school.

Beth is at home with her menagerie of animals and a constant WIFI stream. She is an avid reader and consumer of documentaries who greatly enjoys solving 3D jigsaw puzzles on her VR headset for fun. She loves tech and often helps others or consults on applying it in different situations.

You can find most of Beth's projects at www.sensoryadvice.org

Saving Time By Spending It With Your Kids

By Beth Koenig

Over my life, I have been a nanny, a foster parent, a disabilities rights advocate, an educator, and a consultant working in the special needs space. My work with children has been some of the most rewarding work of my life. I have learned a lot and been able to help the families I worked with quite a lot. I often had to juggle my various responsibilities and help others juggle theirs too. Having more time to spend with their kids is what many women often say is one of the top reasons they want to own their own business. Yet when the pandemic happened in 2020, and many kids and parents were forced to switch to both learning and working from home, there was no preparation nor manual on how to go about things. Teachers tried their best, parents did what they could, and children being the ever adaptable beings they are, either flourished or floundered. Now two years later, I look back on the lessons learned and know that many parents loved spending time with their kids but couldn't figure out how to make it work. At the core, the three main things you need to understand to be able to spend time with your kids and still get your work done are the importance of relationships, early independence, and academics.

The importance of relationships

We have all heard of the importance of the parent-child bond. Children need strong, stable relationships, and that begins in early childhood. The focus of the first three years should be on socializing and building a bond with your child. The time you spend playing with them can teach them essential skills. You can use sign language as you speak and teach words such as "wait" and "freeze," "come," and "go." When introduced in the fun of play, they are easy to learn and come in handy when you need your child to listen to you.

As kids get older, it is vital to continue to spend time with them. Often the busy day can get away from us and make us feel like there is no time to spend with the children. Taking just an extra 10 minutes to let them show you something or talk about something they are interested in really can make all the difference. Your older children would love to connect with you, and one of the best ways to do that is to take an interest in their hobbies. Learn about their favorite games, talk about their favorite TV characters, and the books they have been reading. Find common ground and work on building bonds with them.

Independence

One of the best ways to save your time in business is to delegate things to others. The same holds true at home. You should encourage and teach your children to do things independently as soon as possible. Your two-year-old might lack the fine motor skills to make a sandwich, but he can start learning to take things to his place at the table and "clean up" when he is done eating. A 3 to 4-year-old can learn to pour his own cereal for breakfast and to get his lunch out of the refrigerator. A 5-year-old can also wash dishes, dry them, and put them away. Children can help with the laundry, weed the yard, sweep the floor, and do many other useful things. When they are taught these things from a young age, and you invest the time to teach them, they can be fully independent in their daily living skills sooner than you would expect.

As adults, we often fall into the belief that our children are too young to do something or that they will just make a bigger mess of things. While this is true initially, they will become quite capable as they practice and develop the skills needed to do things. But they will never get there unless you let them practice. We have children who left for college without ever having done their own laundry. Older children who can't seem to keep their room "clean" might lack the skills to do so. Talk with them about what they think might help them to better manage their space. Maybe they would benefit from an extra shelf or some labeled bins. The important thing is to help them find solutions that work for them and not micro-manage their space. At the same time, you don't want that space to be taken over by vermin either. Ideally, their room should take less than fifteen minutes to clean up and vacuum, and they should be able to do it themselves. Make a game out of it using the stopwatch on your phone and offer them something for their best time. You will have to build up to this, but it can be done. Children crave independence; let's let them have more of it!

What about academics?

We all want quality education for our children to prepare them for life. In 2020 education was turned on its head as a pandemic swept the world, leading to widespread lockdowns and school closures. Schools rushed to figure out how to educate children remotely. Unfortunately, children, teachers, and parents were dropped into virtual schooling completely unprepared. Homeschooling, which has been around for 100's of years, was quickly confused with virtual education. Homeschooling can take on many forms and will look different from family to family and even child to child. The great thing about homeschooling is that it can be fully customized for each child. One of the drawbacks of homeschooling is that it can be challenging for families to start because there is so much information.

The first thing you should think about is how your children will do their core academics. Many parents worry about this, but with all of the available tools in technology, there's no reason children can't learn most of their core academics from programs that automatically grade their work and show which skills need to be worked on. This can be a significant timesaver for the busy entrepreneur. You can have your child do their independent work on the computer or tablet and then spend just a little time with them in the evening going over the areas they're having trouble with. Once your core academics are covered, you can look into enrichment activities such as learning a second language, music lessons, etc. Make sure that you ask your child what their interests are, and then create an environment at home that allows them to pursue those interests. They can be busy working on their independent work and pursuing their interests while you're doing your things for your business. Also, for many of the tasks that you do for your business, your children might be able to learn to do and develop important skills in the process. Children can make websites, edit papers, copy and paste information between two different programs, and do many other tasks that an assistant might do for you. This also allows you to spend more time with your children, teaching them how to do the task and helping them learn and grow in their abilities to do it.

One of the most critical skills we can give our children is teaching them to think. Often schools don't teach children to think but rather to memorize in the early years. Our children must learn to think, solve puzzles, and reflect on experiences. All these things will be invaluable as your children get into higher-level academics and other life skills where they have to make difficult decisions.

Often homeschooled children are sent back to regular school for high school by parents that worry they won't be able to teach them; a possible mistake since many homeschooled children are ready to start some college-level work once they finish the 8th grade. As soon as they can write a five-paragraph research essay, they are ready to take college-level coursework that leads to real college credits and credits for high school. Instead of spending four years of high school and then another four at college, children who start college early can often get an AA or BA degree around the same time that they graduate from high school. Even if you don't want to have your child educated at home, you can still set up an enriching home environment that allows them to do many of these things when they're finished with their typical school day.

You will find that as you look at all the things you are doing, spending more time with your kids will help you both save a lot of time!

For more information on educational options for children with or without sensory issues visit http://sensoryadvice.org

ACKNOWLEDGMENTS

This book is in many ways the result of all the incredible and empowering women I have learned from, collaborated with, and connected with over the many years as an aspiring entrepreneur.

Your friendship, your guidance, and your support have made this all possible and I'm truly thankful.

I'm thankful to my bold and brave co-authors, who decided to go on this journey to share their stories of transformation and triumph with openness and genuine heartfelt truth.

Oprah once said, "I've come to believe that each of us has a personal calling that's as unique as a fingerprint — and that the best way to succeed is to discover what you love and then find a way to offer it to others in the form of service, working hard and also allowing the energy of the universe to lead you. "

You have a unique contribution to offer the world, and it's your responsibility to find out what that is. Don't be afraid to embrace your gifts and the things that make you unique.

Create the highest, grandest vision possible for your life because you become what you believe.

Printed in Great Britain
by Amazon

12700646R00119